IN THE SPIRIT OF '76!

THE CITIZEN'S GUIDE TO POLITICS

iN THE SPiRiT OF '76

Third Century Publishers
Washington, D.C.

FIRST PRINTING FEBRUARY 1975
SECOND PRINTING OCTOBER 1975

THIRD CENTURY PUBLISHERS, INC.

Library of Congress Catalogue Number 74-24648

". . . and where the Spirit of the Lord is, there is liberty."

2 Corinthians 3:17

ABOUT THE COVER: The stained glass window depicting George Washington at prayer during the siege of Valley Forge is located in the Protestant Chapel on the U.S. Army Post at Ft. Belvoir, Va. A similar window is located behind the altar of the Prayer Room of the United States Capitol. The window symbolizes the basic unity of belief in God and His Providence that has always characterized the greatness of our nation. Surrounding the figure of General Washington, in the Capitol window, are these words from Psalm 16:1—*"Preserve me, O God: for in Thee do I put my trust"*.

TABLE OF CONTENTS

Foreword

(About The Kind of Book This Is—And Isn't)

This is a book about good government; about politics and political action. A "how to" handbook on winning elections.

Some politicians, and some political professionals, may find it to be too "simple", too basic.

Well, maybe so.

But, this book was not written for them.

There are already a number of books written for them, and by them. Books on how to swing elections. Books on the fast shuffle and the big deal. Texts on how to play one group in society against another; how to manipulate, use mirrors, and win by any means at any price.

This is not that kind of book.

This *is* a book on the basics of effective citizen action. It is written for those Americans—especially Christians—who want America to be truly a government of and by and for the people; based on God's laws and Christ's teachings that were the foundation of this republic.

What better time to do this than now, as we prepare for 1976 and the beginning of this nation's third century!

"In The Spirit of '76" was also written for those Christians who want to get involved in good government and winning campaigns but are not able to afford the services of a professional campaign manager.

It is a handbook for political action primarily designed for use in home and group study courses. The typical course is divided into six parts—one part each week for six weeks:

Week One—"The Christian and Politics", Chapters 1 and 2.

Week Two—"The Basics of Political Organization", Chapters 3 and 4.

Week Three—"The Selection and Building of a Candidate", Chapters 5 and 6.

Week Four—"The Campaign Organization", Chapters 7 and 8.

Week Five—"The Precinct and The Precinct Workers", Chapters 9, 10 and 11.

Week Six—"The Campaign Timetable", Chapters 12 and 13.

Included in *The Appendix* are several sections on additional aspects of campaigning. They are intended as reference material for the study course but they are written in enough detail to be used as specific guides in a campaign.

Hopefully, after you have read this book and completed the course, you will become involved in the affairs of good government in the party or group of your choice. That decision, of course, is up to you. But, every citizen should do what he can, where he is, with what he has—that is the essence of self-government in a republic.

Political action, especially in these times, is important and can be exciting and rewarding—not in a monetary or status-seeking sense but in the knowledge that you are doing your part to rebuild America.

You should also know that politics can be difficult, frustrating and petty—and sometimes even harsh and disappointing.

But, victories, fairly gained, can be sweet.

There will be times when animosity, anger, or scorn will be directed toward you . . . and you will respond with patience, understanding and love. *Because you are God-directed.*

There will be times when your faith will be tested and your temper will be tried. Times when you will be tempted to stretch a point, or twist the truth, or use a lower means to win a vote or gain the victory. But, you will stand fast in faith and refuse to become entangled. *Because you are Christ-centered.*

You will be in politics to win but you will be a Christian in all things . . . *and that will make the difference!*

"In all thy ways acknowledge Him and He will direct thy paths." That is the greatest victory!

CHAPTER ONE

Politics—But Not As Usual

"Christians should get involved in good government."
Dr. Billy Graham

There are some who say that Christians have no business getting involved in politics.

If, by that, they mean politics as usual—the type of politics that seems all too prevalent these days—*they are right.*

But, if they mean politics—the affairs of state, the process by which free men seek the balance between the extremes of anarchy and collectivism—*they are wrong!*

And, if they mean that Christians must divorce themselves from their convictions, or leave their religious beliefs behind when they enter the halls and precincts of government—*they are wrong again.*

Christians have every right to be active in politics. The fact that we love the Lord and have accepted Jesus Christ as our Saviour and Master does not make us second-class citizens or exclude us from the electorate.

Furthermore, Christians have many reasons for taking part in the political processes of civil government. Consider at least these three:

1. The Christian should get into politics to help restore morality and a sense of true values to public affairs. This will help to rebuild public respect and confidence in government.

The vast majority of people today are fed up with politics and government. They have lost faith in the politician. The attitude of the average American toward the politician is akin to contempt. In fact, it is contempt.

One opinion poll asked citizens to rank 20 jobs and professions in order of public esteem and trust. *Politicians ranked 19th*—one rung above used car salesmen.

This aversion to politics and politicians is not new; it is not wholly a by-product of the Watergate scandals. Public distaste began long before that unhappy and unsavory episode. During recent years, volunteer participation in election campaigns has diminished, partisan registration has slipped, and voter turnout at the polls has declined.

Who can blame the citizen for being cynical?

He is wary of the "establishment" and tired of the chicanery in government—at all levels.

He is sick of being bought off with his own money; distressed and discouraged at the red tape and remoteness of government; disgruntled over the inflation that destroys his earnings, and downright mad about the taxes—taxes for all governments, federal, state and local—that take almost 43 percent of all the personal income earned in the United States. *Forty-three percent!* The Lord asks ten percent; Caesar and his legions are not so easily satisfied.

And, even with the huge tax grab the nation's problems worsen as government grows even bigger and its budgets go further into debt. Is it any wonder that public opinion pollsters find that most Americans feel politics is self-serving and government is irresponsive, irresponsible and irrelevant?

A Phillips-Sindlinger survey, taken in March, 1974, reported that only 26 percent of Americans gave the federal congress a positive rating on the way it handles national affairs. A September, 1974 Harris poll gave Congress even lower marks (18%) and surveys at the state level reflect the same general antagonism toward the legislatures.

Several years ago, on a day when its members were wrestling

with a seven billion dollar annual budget, Dr. Billy Graham addressed a joint session of the California State Legislature. He reminded the lawmakers that the problems of California—and America—were not just economic but also moral and spiritual. He suggested that both the human spirit and the national soul were perhaps more in need of repair than the budget.

The fact is that many of the so-called political issues of our day are not political, *they are moral.*

Warned Dr. Graham: "Morals are sinking with every passing hour. If they sink much lower, democracy cannot survive. Without morality, America will head straight into the arms of a dictator."

Only moral citizens can restore morality to government; in the long haul government is, indeed, a mirror of its people.

2. Christians should get active in public affairs because government is involved in virtually every aspect of our daily lives.

Former Congressman Walter H. Judd, for years a Christian medical missionary in China, put it this way:

"No one will deny that today our national government is the most powerful force and factor in the lives of most American citizens, businesses, organizations, and enterprises.

"The conditions under which an employer deals with his employees, his competitors, and now his customers, are more and more determined by Washington. The conditions under which employees deal with their employers, or with their unions, is the same.

"How much a person can earn, how much he can keep of what he is able to earn, and how much that will buy—all these are increasingly determined by the actions of the Congress, the Executive, and the administrative agencies."

Dr. Judd was speaking of the federal government. He might have gone on to observe that the state and local governments add *their* restraints and constraints, *their* rules and regulations, on top of that.

Raymond Moley, author, teacher, and advisor to four Presidents, once commented that government is with us from the moment we are born until the day our mortal remains are lowered into the ground.

Wrote Dr. Moley: "Politics lays a heavy hand on every circumstance of our lives.

"It can measurably tell us what job we may have and what we may get for our labors. It takes our children and decrees what they shall be taught. It can take our youth and destroy them in war. It can enter our dwellings and seize our private effects. If we go on as we have, it will regiment our lives from conception to dissolution. Even our quiet graves are made to specifications drawn by a bureaucrat.

"We must master politics or be mastered by those who do."

Consider the onslaught of big government since Dr. Moley wrote those words in 1957.

And, consider this: *freedom is indivisible!*

The government that controls the individual's endeavors in other areas—economics, education, labor, trade, travel and politics—must sooner or later control the individual's freedom of religion.

How can Christians afford not to get involved?

3. Christians should get involved in government because Divine Guidance is the only power that can restore the soul of this nation and save it from a terrible disaster or even total destruction.

Who can deny that these are darkening days?

The smaller this globe grows, the more it seems to fly apart. There are wars and rumors of war; hot wars, cold wars, brush wars and economic wars. There are famine and hunger, disease and suffering, strife and turmoil. There is financial uncertainty bordering on a chaos that could serve as the prelude to an awful world-wide depression with its untold human misery. It would seem the "distress of the nations" is upon us.

It is not so much that we fear for ourselves; it is that as Christians we love our fellowmen and we do, indeed, fear for their future.

Dr. Judd, drawing on his years as a Christian missionary and his knowledge as a former congressman, makes this analysis of the world situation:

"What our government in Washington does depends more than ever before on what happens, or may happen, in Central Europe, the Middle East, Southeast Asia, parts of Africa and Latin America. Much of what happens in those places depends on decisions in Moscow, Peking, Hanoi and Havana. And, the decisions in those places still depend to a greater extent than we realize, I think, on what we in the United States do in our role as citizens—or, what they think we will do.

"Therefore, it is more imperative than at any time since the founding of our Republic that citizens pay attention to and become involved in the processes that determine what our government is to do, at home and abroad."

On the eve of his inauguration to his first term as President of the United States, Dwight D. Eisenhower was moved to assert:

"America must have a religious revival if it is to survive."

That was in early 1952. The passing of time has accelerated since then.

In his splendid essay, "You Are Responsible",* John B. Conlan, the dynamic young congressman from Phoenix, Arizona, addressed his fellow-Christians in America:

"This is a spiritual battle, against principalities, powers, rulers of darkness.

"You are responsible for the future course of our nation and its relations with the nations of the world. You are responsible for maintaining our freedom. You are responsible for preventing the grip of decadent socialism upon our land. You are responsible for selecting your government and your leaders.

"You and I are responsible to build a nation in keeping with basic Christian principles.

"The Lord put the challenge this way: 'I sought for a man among them, that should make up the hedge, and stand in the gap before me for the land, that I should not destroy it; *but I found none*' (Ezekiel 22:30)."

And then Mr. Conlan raised the question:

"Will that be America's epitaph because Christians were too busy . . .?"

Is it too late now? Too late for Christians to get involved; too late to turn things around? It is never too late to be about The Lord's work!

Second Chronicles 7:14 holds God's promise:

"*If* my people, which are called by my name, shall humble themselves and pray, and seek my face, and turn from their wicked

---

* *"You Are Responsible"*, Rep. John B. Conlan, American Tract Society, Oradell, New Jersey.

ways; *then will I hear from heaven, and will forgive their sins, and will heal their land."*

The prophet Samuel makes it clear that *people do, indeed, get the kind of government and government officials they resemble.* Samuel warns us that if we ignore the will of The Lord and walk in our own appetites, we will have leaders who do the same. But, "if you will fear The Lord and serve Him and obey His voice, and will not rebel against His way, both you and the king (*or president, or governor, or congressman*) who reigns over you will certainly be God's followers". (I Samuel 12:14)

What more do we need to encourage us, to motivate us, to become active in the *healing* of our land?

A Little Bit of Leaven

And yet, some of our Christian friends will continue to insist that they just cannot bring themselves to get into political action.

"It's a dirty business. I want no part of *that."*

Well, no Christian does.

And that is exactly why Christians must get into political action: *to clean things up!* Not to conform, *but to transform!*

Carl F. H. Henry, lecturer-at-large for World Vision International and former editor of *Christianity Today,* issued this warning to the non-participant:

"The call for Christian participation in political life is grounded not simply in the moral and spiritual chaos of the modern nations, but in a biblical mandate as well. Christians should be politically active . . . to the limit of their ability and competence.

"The penalty for failure to lead and to be vocal is that others, who misuse and exploit political power for objectionable ends and objectionable means, pre-empt the field."

Christians can succeed in politics without playing dirty. They do not leave their faith and their ethics behind when they become involved in the affairs of government. *God First,* always, in all things—that is the basis on which Christians get involved in any activity—spiritual, or secular.

To say that a Christian cannot be active in politics without getting dirty, or being dirty, is to belittle the sustaining power of our faith and to suggest that God can prevail in some areas, but not all.

If that attitude were to prevail, Christians would withdraw from the world—from commerce, and law, and sports, and medicine; from education and journalism, and whatever else. Politics is not the only arena in the human contest where the game gets tough and some get rough. There are unholy pressures in virtually every aspect of life. Should we therefore refrain from entering such professions, or trades, or avocations? Certainly not!

Jesus said, *"I pray that Thou shalt not take them out of the world . . As Thou has sent me into the world, even so have I sent them into the world."* (John 17:15,18)

What we must do is participate with energy and skill and refuse to be a party to any dirty deals or questionable pursuits or practices.

Be *in* the world—*but not of* the world. Meaning, just because you're in Rome should not cause you to do as the Romans may do. When in "Rome", or politics, or whatever and wherever, do as a Christian should do. Stand fast in your faith, fight the good fight; be consistent in your good works, with love and understanding . . . *like the yeast that leavens the loaf and raises the level of all it touches.*

"Do unto others as you would have them do unto you."

What a tremendous transformation would occur if the *Golden Rule* were applied to politics and government!

Can you imagine the change that would be wrought? *No more political campaigns based on "victory at any price by any means". No more dog-eat-dog tactics. no more under-the-table deals. No more false witness. No more ego trips for self-centered purposes. Where there is now animosity, there would be love; where there is greed there would be generosity and compassion. Patience would take the place of anger and service would rise above self.*

We could put the corrupt practices act and the campaign disclosure laws into a museum along with other relics of a by-gone era. Holding public office would be akin to entering the priesthood.

Consider this: if Christians had become active in politics ten years ago—or, five years ago—and if we had in all things been faithful to God's commandments and Christ's teachings, what a wonderful government we would have today!

CHAPTER TWO

Let's Get Started!

"You are responsible for selecting your government and civic leaders! And if you say you are not responsible, then who is?"

Rep. John B. Conlan
Member of Congress

If politics is people, and it is, then politics should be you. Let's get started!

How do you get going in politics? It's easy. There are several routes you can go.

You probably already know someone in your neighborhood or among your friends who is active in politics—either in an official party organization, or in some volunteer political group, or in a candidate's campaign. Give them a call. Tell them you want to become active.

You have taken the first step!

Perhaps there is no one in your neighborhood, no one in your circle of friends or acquaintances, who is active with the political party you prefer, or the candidate of your choice, or a ballot proposition that turns you on. If that's the case, it is a clear indication that there is plenty of room for you in the area in which you want to get active.

In fact, if you have never had a house call, or a phone call, or any kind of contact on behalf of your party or your candidate, there is a real need for your participation!

So, Take the Plunge!

Here are some of the ways you can make political contact:

1. *Call your party's local headquarters.* In most counties and in many cities the party maintains an office with a listed phone number.

Give a call. Tell the secretary or the chairman or the person who answers the phone who you are, where you live and that you would like to get active. The odds are they will greet you with open arms and a job to do.

The same thing goes for a candidate's committee or a citizen's group working on a ballot issue. (Since such organizations are "temporary", be sure to check with "Information" for a telephone listing.)

If you are a shut-in and can't get out of the house, there are many jobs you can do for your candidate or party—right in your own home: helping with mailings (lickin' and stickin' and stuffin'), making phone calls to recruit volunteers, checking precinct registration lists, etc.

2. If there is no listing for the party or the candidate's committee in your area, *call the local newspaper or radio station.*

Usually someone in the newsroom can direct you to a local party official. If that doesn't work, call the county clerk or registrar of voters. Someone in that office should be able to give you the name of your party chairman or an official in your area.

3. If all else fails, there are at least two more things you can do:

—call one of the *elected officials* in your area who is a member of your party or call the *district office of your congressman* if he is of the party of your choice.

—keep an eye open for *political news* in your local newspaper. When an article appears quoting or referring to an individual as a party spokesman or official, give that person a call.

Remember this: usually it is not difficult to make contact with someone in the party of your choice, or someone in the campaign or office of the candidate of your choice. *But,* the more difficult it is, the more your help is needed and the greater the opportunity for you to get active and be effective.

Here's another thought.

Instead of going it alone, why not get several of your like-minded friends or neighbors to go along with you. Can you imagine what would happen if four or five of you walked into a party head-quarters, or a candidate's campaign office, and announced, "Hi! We live out in the _____ area and we'd like to do some work for you."

On Your Own

Perhaps you and your friends can't "buy" either party or any of the candidates. Perhaps the volunteer groups don't turn you on. It could be the political activists in your area are more interested in party-parties and social events than public affairs.

You can still be effectively active in politics.

There are literally millions of citizens who don't like the way things are going, either. They, like you, believe that a transformation is vital in politics and government.* You probably know some folks like that—in your church, your Bible class, your service club or civic organization; individuals who want to get politics back to principles and government back on track. Many of them are probably God-centered Americans.

There is your opportunity to do something—to make a difference in politics, and in America. Get in touch with those individuals. Start an informal study group. Use this text and its supplemental materials as the discussion guide. Then, branch out into precinct work; take on an issue or support a candidate. Participate!

---

* The Gallup Poll of July 18, 1974, reported that 33% of the American public considered itself politically *Independent;* a continuation of a shift away from the parties that began in the early 1960s. Among voters under 30, 47% said they were Independent, a shift of 7% since 1972.

A Word About Study Groups

Door-to-door precinct work has been the traditional foundation of political effort. In many areas, it still is. However, in an increasing number of neighborhoods, house-to-house political work is becoming a thing of the past—unless the political volunteer has established himself, or herself, as a good and trusted friend.

Consider, for example, the impact of the rising crime rate. Many homeowners tend to view any stranger at their door with suspicion, fear and even hostility. And, many volunteers who were once willing to walk a precinct now refuse to take to the streets out of fear for their personal safety.

Add to that the public cynicism toward politics. Many citizens have turned off to politicians and political workers. Ask yourself: what would be your reaction if a stranger knocked on your door on behalf of a political party or candidate?

Today, to be effective, politics must be personalized. Political work must be done by individuals who are the friends or trusted acquaintances of those they call upon.

The neighborhood study group is one of the best ways to achieve that acceptance; that is why it can become one of the most important units in contemporary political action.

Actually, the study group is not a new concept. The idea of friends and like-minded neighbors getting together to review and discuss an issue of mutual concern is part of the American tradition. And today, for example, literally millions of Americans are already meeting in weekly neighborhood Bible study groups. Since the effort for good government is one more extension and application of Christian citizenship, the idea of neighborhood good government study groups now takes on added importance.

This book is designed to help like-minded citizens get involved in politics through getting involved in neighborhood study groups. Its purpose is to assist you in your efforts to rebuild the American system of representative democracy—a government of and by and for the people, bottom to top!

It is based on the concept of the ever-expanding circle—the ever-growing spheres of influence that start with the Christ-centered individual and radiate outward in love and interest and influence.

As your study group grows in size and strength, encourage members to spin off and form their own study fellowships in their block, or their precinct. Imagine the impact that could be generated if there were a study group in each precinct within your legislative or congressional district! Obviously, as the number of individuals in these study groups increases, the number of personal contacts throughout the precinct—and district—*is multiplied.*

This book devotes three chapters to precinct organization and duties. The effectiveness—the winning ways—of those chapters could be multiplied many-fold by basing your precinct organization and operation on a foundation of these good government study groups. It can be done with a minimum of time and effort—four to six hours each month, starting in the off-election year. That is not really a lot of time to give, not nearly what our founding fathers gave . . . *and not nearly what many of our sons and husbands and brothers have given in the service of the nation!*

Local Issues and Officials

Say "elections" to the average citizen and he thinks mostly of national and state elections. Once in awhile you'll find someone who mentions local (city, county and special district) elections.

That's why there is such a voter drop-off between the top and the bottom of the ballot. Usually there is a drop of about five percent between the vote for the President and the vote for U.S. Senator (say, from 70% down to 65%). And, another drop from Senator to Representative (say from 65% to 62%). By the time you get down to the end of the ballot—to the Judges and the County Clerk, or whatever—the drop-off is as much as ten percent.

It's the same with off-year and local elections. In a Presidential election year, the turnout of *registered voters* may be as high as 75 percent. On a non-Presidential year, it may drop as low as 55-60 percent and for odd-year local elections it may fall as low as 40, and even 30, percent.

The "arithmetic of politics" in America is sad enough at the national and congressional level (see Chapter Four). It is even more tragic at the local level; often as few as 15 or 20 percent of the adult population—and frequently less than 30 percent—select the men and women who control our local governments and governmental agencies. The policies of hundreds—thousands—of local school districts are determined by men and women who were put into office by five percent of the electorate, or less!

In viewing the political scene, look at it from the bottom up; from the school district to the city council to the county board to the state legislature to the congress to the statewide offices. There are no doubt local problems that demand attention; things that need setting straight not just in your state capitol or in Washington but in your town and your county.

If some of the state and federal issues that bug us now had been solved at the local levels years ago they would not now be millstones around our public neck. *And, remember this:* political problems that are ignored or neglected often return as moral issues . . . and those we cannot ignore.

So, whether it's an incumbent who has gone sour, or a vacancy on the city council or in the Congress—let's do something about it. Let's get started.

Contact your friends. Call the neighbors along the street. Get your friends from church or Bible class. All those folks you know who are upset, in general, and angry, in particular, about some specific situation.

Give them a call. Invite them over for coffee some evening this week, or next. Put it to them this way:

"Look! We've been complaining about (such-and-such, or so-and-so) long enough. Why don't we do something about it?

"Bill and George and Barbara and several of the rest of us have been talking it over and we have some ideas we'd like to suggest. You folks probably have some thoughts, too. Maybe yours are better. Whatever, why don't we get together and start a study group? Let's get the rest of the neighborhood (or club or class or congregation) to join us and get to work.

"If we could all get together on this, we could clear things up (or, elect a good councilman, or legislator or congressman)."

The first thing you know, you have the seeds of a citizen's group. And if you keep at it your enthusiasm and effort can spread and increase in size and impact . . . like the tiny mustard seed that, in its season, can populate a hillside with its dancing, yellow light.

Faith, persistence, a compelling message—that is political action at its best!

A Family Affair

Incidentally, a word of advice: make your politics a family affair.

Constructive political action can be a real education for the kids. They'll get a kick out of it, too. Why not start them in a study group of their own?

More importantly, make politics a family affair because the family is the basic unit—*God's basic unit, freedom's basic unit.* The family is the foundation of a healthy society.

We defeat the purpose of working for good government if we permit our political activities to weaken our family ties. What do we really gain if we elect the "right" individual to office but cause parents to drift apart from each other, or their children?

Christian families pray and worship together, play and work together, and grow together . . . and we would do well to make politics together, too!

CHAPTER THREE

The Structure of Politics

"The political parties which I style great are those which cling to principles more than to their consequences; to general, and not to especial, cases; to ideas, and not to men. These parties are usually distinguished by a nobler character, by more generous passions, more genuine convictions, and a more bold and open conduct . . ."

Alexis de Tocqueville

From the beginning, the American republic has employed the dynamics of the free market system to provide the greatest good for the greatest number of people. It has cultivated this open competition between individuals to create, produce, distribute and sell those products and services the people need and desire.

The same tradition of free and constructive competition has given us our political system; an arrangement through which political parties vie for public approval and support through their programs, policies and candidates.

In a sense, politics is simply the marketing of ideas regarding the operation of our government, and the selling of candidates who will implement those ideas. Just as manufacturers compete for public favor—*and sales*—through price and quality, so the political parties compete for public favor—*and votes*—through programs, policies and candidates.

27

Now that you have decided to get involved in government—and politics—you should take time to learn something about the basic structure of politics. How the parties are organized, how they operate, and what they are supposed to do. Even if your political efforts are going to be nonpartisan, knowing these things will help you to be more effective.

Political Structure

To put it simply, the structure of the major political parties in the United States parallels the various levels of government—federal, state and local.

The parties' *national committees* concern themselves primarily with matters pertaining to the federal government (the election of President and Vice President, national platforms, national and international issues, etc.).

The *state committees* are mostly concerned with affairs of the government at that level (the election of statewide officials—Governor, Lt. Governor, U. S. Senators, etc., state platforms, state issues, state legislative matters, etc.).

The *local committees* (county and district and sometimes city or town) look after the political concerns at that level and work to elect their candidates to public office in the various subdivisions involved.

Both parties also maintain national *senatorial and congressional* campaign committees to coordinate the various efforts (research, fund-raising, publicity, etc.) designed to elect or re-elect their candidates. Some state legislators have formed partisan *legislative campaign committees* to assist them in their elections.

National Committees

The national committee of each party comprises two members from each state—a national committeeman and a national committeewoman. The Republicans also include on their national committee the party chairman from each of the 50 states.

National committee members are selected (nominated) by the party at the state levels (either through a vote of the victorious presidential delegation or by the membership of the state committee).

What are the duties of the national committee?

The committee is charged with the operation of the party's national (presidential nominating) convention. It may call other conventions and meetings to conduct the party's national business.

The national committee also elects the party's national officers. However, the chairman and co-chairman are usually chosen by the party's presidential candidate and acceptance by the committee is traditional. The national chairman serves as the party spokesman; this is particularly important if his party is out of power because in such circumstances he expresses the view of the loyal opposition.

Finally, the national committee works in tandem with the party's presidential candidate's committee to conduct nationwide campaigns and oversees the operations of the party's national headquarters and staff. It conducts major fund-raising efforts (such as the Democratic party's national telethon).

Political Structure At The State Level

Our federal constitution does not mention or make provisions for political parties. That was left up to the people and to the several states. Thus, the structure and operation of political parties may differ widely from state to state.

Each state has its own set of election codes to govern the basic political organizations within its boundaries. In addition, state party organizations adopt various rules and by-laws that spell out the fundamental principles of structure and operation.

What is presented in this section is a general review of typical party structure and operation at the state level. More complete details on how the parties are structured in your state will be found in the *supplemental manual on your state* that was published in conjunction with this text.

State Committees

The highest level of official party structure in each state is the state (central) committee.

In some states the membership of the state committee comprises:

—*the party's nominees* for all partisan public offices

—*the appointees of those nominees* (as alloted by law)

—*the state chairmen* (or presidents) *of the party's major volunteer groups,* and

—all or some of the *chairmen of the party's county committees.*

In other states committee members are elected at the local level, in precinct or district conventions. The supplemental manual on your state has those details.

The state committee conducts the party's business at the state level, including:

—direction of *statewide campaigns* in support of the party's candidates (including special get-out-the-vote efforts, etc.)

—the operation of the party's *state headquarters* and the hiring and supervision of a professional staff

—*fund-raising efforts* to finance the statewide campaigns and to finance the party's housekeeping operations, and

—the convening of *official party meetings* as required by law and as deemed necessary by the committee's leadership.

In some states, the state committee drafts and adopts the party platform; in other states that chore is given to a special state convention comprising the party's nominees for all partisan public offices.

As a general rule, the state committee may not endorse candidates in a contested primary election. Its political campaign functions are usually confined to the general elections on behalf of the nominees selected in the party primaries. However, there are notable exceptions, such as Ohio, with official party pre-primary endorsement conventions.

County Committees

The major duty of the county committee is to *carry the county for the party*--in other words, to elect its candidates to office and to gain a majority of the votes in the county for the party's statewide and district candidates.

It works to achieve that goal through
  —raising *campaign funds* (that are apportioned among local, district and state candidates)
  —mounting sustained, year-round *public information programs* to sway the voters
  —putting on *voter registration drives,* and
  —building the strongest possible *precinct organization* to deliver the vote on election day (including the coordination of the efforts of the party's volunteer groups).

Membership on the county committee varies by state. In some states, the county committee members are elected at specially called meetings (caucuses, mass meetings or conventions). In other states, the county committee members are elected by supervisorial or legislative district or by precinct. Elections for those offices are held at the primary on even-numbered years. Each district or precinct is alloted a predetermined number of committee members, based on the voter population within that area.

Committee members elect a chairman and other officers. The chairman, in turn, selects the members of the executive committee and the members of the various standing committees (finance, precinct organization, publicity, headquarters operations, etc.).

Local Committees

In some states, the official party organization structure extends all the way to the local (town or city) level. Such is usually the case where the local officials (city councilmen, mayor, city clerk, etc.) are elected on a partisan basis.

The local party committee is generally composed of the precinct leaders within the town or city. These precinct leaders are elected by their peers--the registered voters of that party in their precinct. If the precincts are then combined into wards, for organizational or operational purposes, the ward leader becomes a member of the party's town or city executive committee.

The Precinct

The precinct is the basic building block, the vital unit, in politics. It is the foundation of political organization; here the party lives or dies and elections are won or lost.

There is nothing magical about the way precincts are established. The precinct is a geographical area arbitrarily drawn by county election officials on the basis of the number of citizens of voting age; the aim is to have roughly the same voting population in each precinct. This enables the election officials to locate convenient polling places at election time and assists them in gathering and tabulating the votes cast.

It also provides the political parties with a logical base on which to build their organization and it gives the individual political worker a well-defined and manageable area of operations and opportunity. *The precinct is the market place of practical politics.*

The Precinct Leader

The precinct leader is responsible for organizing his or her precinct for the party and delivering the party's vote on election day.

In some states the precinct leader (or, captain) is elected by the members of the party residing within that precinct. In other states, the precinct leader volunteers his or her services or is recruited by the party's county committee. Whatever the method, one thing is sure:

The precinct leader and his or her workers are the foot soldiers of the political campaigns.

Candidates and committees may bombard the voter with high-priced media, they may "soften the ground" with advertising and promotion and publicity, they may hold spectacular rallies and make stirring speeches—all of that is an important part of any campaign. *But, in the final analysis, victory or defeat depends on the precinct worker.*

Did the precinct worker do the job, day-after-day and week-after-week, to build rapport and confidence with the voters on her street or in his apartment house? Did she "sell" them on her candidate or her party? Did he get them registered to vote? Did she get them out to vote on election day?

Those are the most important questions in politics. Before you can make a difference in Washington, or the state house or the courthouse, *you must make a difference in your precinct.*

"Unofficial" Partisan Groups

Individual citizens often join together to form "unofficial" partisan political organizations. Quite often such groups spring into being when the official party organization resembles a "closed shop" or when the party fails to give sufficient consideration to the viewpoint of a large bloc of its constituents.

Sometimes these volunteer, or "unofficial", groups are tied to the candidacy of one man, such as the "Citizens for Eisenhower".

Others, such as the California Republican Assembly (CRA) or the California Democratic Council (CDC), are formed to promote a particular political viewpoint within the party family. Generally, those who form or join such organizations are issue-oriented; motivated more by political philosophy and idealism than by personality cults or a drive for personal power or prestige. Quite often these groups are successful in swaying the official party organization toward their viewpoint on issues and programs.

The most important activity of the unofficial group is its *pre-primary endorsements* and election campaign efforts on behalf of its favored candidates. Since the official party generally remains neutral in contested primary elections, the unofficial (or "irregular") groups can often have a disproportionate influence on the outcome of those elections.

Customarily the volunteer groups cooperate with the regular party organization after the primary and during the general election campaigns. Members of the unofficial groups join in the major voter-registration and get-out-the-vote drives, including special "victory squad" efforts on election day. Republicans tend to have the greater number of volunteer (or "unofficial") groups. Democrats traditionally have looked to organized labor, and its various political action arms, for assistance in voter campaigns and precinct work.

Typical State
POLITICAL PARTY STRUCTURE
(See chart on opposite page)

Party organization varies by state. Check your state manual for the way your party is structured in your state. This chart depicts a typical structure found in many states. In it, the party voters elect (either through the party primary or a convention) the members of the county central committee. County committee members can be elected from legislative districts, precincts, or wards. The county committee elects its chairman and generally he selects the members of the executive committee. The committee also selects its representatives to the state committee. Larger counties are often divided into congressional or legislative district committees to oversee party business, conduct campaigns, and select members to the state committee. Smaller counties frequently join to form a campaign committee for their common congressional district.

The state committee customarily comprises representatives of the county and congressional district committees plus elected public officials and/or their appointees, national committee members, heads of the party's volunteer groups, county chairmen, and the special appointees of the state chairman. In some states, party members vote directly in the primary for state committee members. Some state committees wield full party authority; in other states, county committees are virtually autonomous.

Typical State

POLITICAL PARTY STRUCTURE

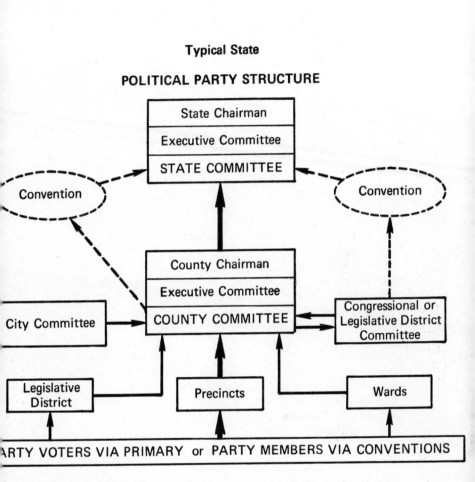

"Third Force Groups"

Although they are not often found in any organizational chart, "third force" groups are an important part of the American political system. These are independent forces, usually representing a special interest. Their purpose is to influence the political parties and the political process and they attempt to do this in various ways:

Lobbying activities at the federal and state capitols, contributions of money and manpower in election campaigns, "wining and dining" legislators and other officials, etc.

Some of the more prominent third force entities on today's political scene are:

ACA—Americans for Constitutional Action
ACLU—American Civil Liberties Union
ACU—American Conservative Union
ADA—Americans for Democratic Action
American Farm Bureau Federation
AM-PAC—the political action arm of the American Medical Association
BI-PAC—Business and Industry Political Action Committee
Chamber of Commerce of the United States
Common Cause
COPE—the political action arm of the AFL-CIO
DRIVE—the political action arm of the Teamsters Union
NAACP—National Association for the Advancement of Colored People
NAM—National Association of Manufacturers
National Council of Churches
NEA—National Education Association
The Sierra Club

That is only a short listing of the many third force groups active on the national political scene today. Similar special interest groups are at work in almost every one of the 50 states and in many of the 3,044 counties throughout the nation.

CHAPTER FOUR

The Arithmetic of Politics

"Taken in one big lump, the idea of winning an election may seem formidable and the odds insurmountable. But, if you really look at politics you see that it's mostly a matter of numbers!"

Hon. Robert Burke
California State Assembly

Our forefathers—those men who founded this Republic—meant for the United States to be governed by the will of the majority as expressed through free and orderly elections.

But, it doesn't always work that way. *Not really!*

A review of recent political history will demonstrate this. Check the vital statistics of 1972 elections as a case in point.

In that year, 1972, slightly more than one-half—56 percent—of all Americans of voting age bothered to cast a ballot in the Presidential election. *The other 44 percent—almost 61 million Americans—didn't even bother to register to vote or go to the polls!*

Here is the record:

Americans of voting age	139.6 million	(100%)
Those registered to vote	92.7 "	(74%)
Those who voted for a presidential candidate	78.9 "	(56%)
Those who voted for Mr. Nixon	47.1 "	(34%)
Those who did not vote	*60.7 million*	*(44%)*

Study the bottom line in that table:

There were more adult Americans *not* voting for a president in 1972 than all those who voted for the winning candidate!

Only one out of every three citizens of voting age had a hand in selecting the Chief Executive to guide the destinies of this nation. *One out of three!* That is not the will of the majority; that is the will of *one-third* of the citizens.

Congressional Races

The fact that a minority of voters can and often does determine the make up of our federal government can be seen even more clearly in the results of the 1974 congressional elections—elections that seated 435 men and women in the U.S. House of Representatives.

Less than one-third—*only 30 percent*—of all Americans of voting age bothered to vote in those elections!

Here are the data:

Americans of voting age	144.9 million	(100%)
Those who voted for a congressional representative	43.5 "	(30%)
Those who did not vote	*101.4 million*	(70%)
Those who voted Democrat	24.3 "	(17%)

In 1974, Americans who did not bother to vote for congressional representation outnumbered those who did by more than two to one! And, only seventeen percent—*less than one in five*—of all adult Americans decided that the Democrats should hold a two-thirds majority control of the House of Representatives—the House of Congress that supposedly most directly reflects the philosophy and will of all the people.

State Elections

It's pretty much the same at the state level. Take June 4, 1974, as an example. On that day they held an election in California *and less than half the people came.* Only 47.3 percent bothered to vote. The rest stayed home, or went shopping, or swimming, or something.

And, look what happened:

• 19 percent of all the registered Democrats *(less than one in five)* selected that party's nominee for governor; about one out of eight (13 percent) chose the Democrat nominee for Secretary of State.

• 32 percent of the registered Republicans in California *(less than one in three)* selected that party's nominee for governor and less than one out of seven (14 percent) picked the GOP nominee for Secretary of State.

• 28 percent of all the registered voters—2.8 million individuals—saddled all 20.5 million Californians with the likelihood of an additional $250 million in long-term bonded indebtedness.

That is no way to run a state. It's no way to run a republic. For a republic to work, the people must take part in the affairs of their government.

GRASS ROOTS MATH

The year 1974 was not really an unusual year as far as the low percentage of voter turnout in congressional elections. In 1970 only 43.5 percent of the voting age population cast a ballot for congress; in 1966, 45.4 percent; and, back in 1954, only 41.7 percent.

So, let's take a 50 percent voter turn out and apply it at the local level, to the precinct.

Let's apply it on the basis of a precinct with 100 adults who could vote if they bothered to register and go to the polls. Granted, most precincts have more than 100 potential voters, but using the figure 100 will help make a point. In fact, it will help to make two points:

First, it will illustrate how few people take advantage of the right to participate in government, and

Second, it will demonstrate the great opportunity that exists if you are willing to work your precinct and get out your vote.

Here's how our precinct table looks:

Citizens of voting age	100
Those registered to vote	74
(Those NOT registered)	*26*
Those who voted	50
(Those NOT voting)	*50*

Let's go deeper. Let's apply those statistics to a primary election in a precinct in which the partisan registration is 60 percent Democratic and 40 percent Republican (a typical three-to-two edge for Democrats).

	Dem.	Rep.	Total
Voting age pop.	60	40	100
Those registered	44	30	74
Those *not* registered	16	10	26
Those voting	30	20	50
Those *not* voting	30	20	50
Votes to win primary	*16*	*11*	. . .

By The Numbers!

In a manner of speaking, precinct politics is a matter of numbers: *getting the maximum number of persons to vote for your candidate.* Getting at least 50 percent of the vote cast, plus one, gives you the victory.

If every one in our hypothetical precinct of 100 voters were to register and vote, it would require 31 votes to win a Democratic primary, and 21 to win the Republican primary. *But, only 50 percent bother to register and vote.* Thus, it would take only 16 votes to win the Democratic primary and only 11 votes to win the Republican nomination.

Only eleven votes!

Let's suppose that you are a Republican worker in that precinct. How would you go about getting at least 11 votes for your candidate in a primary election?

There are at least three ways to go:

1. At least 10 Republicans in that precinct *were not* registered to vote. How many of those 10 can you get registered?

2. Another 20 Republicans were registered but *did not bother*

to vote in the past election. Can you get half of them to the polls this time? How many can you get?

3. Of the 20 Republicans who did vote last time, *how many can you "sell" on your candidate?*

Remember: you need only 11 votes—*only 11 percent of all the voting population in your precinct*—and your candidate carries that precinct. Start with yourself, that's one vote. How about your spouse? That's another vote. What about your neighbors on either side? Maybe that's another two or four votes, right there. And, those good friends down the street. And so it goes. One by one, vote by vote, you get your eleven votes and you carry your precinct for your candidate.

In the meantime, the precinct worker in the adjacent precinct is doing the same thing. And, the worker in the next, and the next. That is how districts are carried and that's how elections are won! Vote by vote, precinct by precinct, *one by one.*

All of the data used above have been hypothetical, of course. But, the analysis is real. Why not get the data on your precinct and analyze them. Find out what it would take to win a primary. Or, a general election. How many votes would you need? Where could you get them?

There are three chapters in this book devoted to the organization, the working, and the care and leading of *precincts.* Master those and you can master politics—*and win elections!*

ONLY ONE?

Elections are won in the precincts and precincts are won by workers who get out their votes—*one by one.*

Just one vote? With thousands and hundreds of thousands and millions of voters voting, how can just one vote be important?

Well, every year in this nation hundreds of elections are won—or lost—*by just one vote per precinct.* Some, in fact, have been lost—or won—*by less than one vote per precinct;* some by less than one vote *per county!* Here are a few from the record book:

- In 1974 the outcome of U.S. Senate seats in both New Hampshire and North Dakota were so close (10 votes in N.H. and 16 votes in N.D.) that both parties made challenges and counter-challenges and demands for recounts. It was weeks before the winners were finally certified.
- *Nevada, 1974*—Paul Laxalt defeated Harry Reid by 615 votes and was elected to the U.S. Senate by *less than one vote* in each of that state's 930 precincts.
- *Ohio, 1974*—James Rhodes defeated incumbent John Gilligan and was elected Governor by a margin of about 10,000 votes; *less than one vote* in each of Ohio's 12,800 precincts.
- *Nebraska, 1974*—Virginia Smith won election to the U.S. House of Representatives by some 800 votes—a margin of less than one vote in each of the Third District's 864 precincts.
- *California, 1974*—Congressman Vic Veysey was defeated in his re-election bid in the 35th CD by a margin of less than one vote per precinct.
- *Pennsylvania, 1974*—in a special election in the 12th Congressional District, John Murtha defeated Harry Fox by a total of 122 votes. There were 430 precincts in the district. Murtha won by a margin of *one-fourth of a vote* per precinct!
- *Kentucky, 1970*—Roman Mazzoli was elected to the U. S. House of Representatives by *two-thirds of a vote* per precinct.
- *Oregon, 1968*—Robert Packwood defeated incumbent U. S. Senator Wayne Morse by a margin of *1.1* votes per precinct.
- *South Dakota, 1962*—George McGovern was elected to the U. S. Senate by *far less than one vote* per precinct.
- *U.S.A. 1960*—John F. Kennedy defeated Richard M. Nixon by 113,000 votes. That was about *one-half vote* per precinct.
- *U.S.A., 1958*—six congressmen were re-elected to the House of Representatives, each by *less than one vote* per precinct.
- *Texas, 1948*—Lyndon B. Johnson was elected to the U. S. Senate by 87 votes out of 988,295 votes cast in 6,000 precincts. *That figures out to 1/69th of a vote per precinct!*
  . . . and, in 1918, Woodrow Wilson carried the state of California by *less than one vote* per precinct. California's electoral vote *made the difference;* Wilson was re-elected President.
  Who said one vote doesn't count!

CHAPTER FIVE

Finding The Best Candidate

"God give us men! A time like this demands
Strong minds, great hearts, true faith and ready hands;
Men whom the lust of office does not kill!
Men whom the spoils of office cannot buy;
Men who possess opinions and a will:
Men who have honor; men who will not lie."
Dr. J. G. Holland

In a very real sense, the candidate we elect to public office is us—*by proxy;* whether he is on the city council, or in the state legislature or the federal congress.

Since we-the-people cannot spend full-time on the affairs of our government we elect others to serve as our representatives, to reflect our views, to state our positions, to protect our interests and to use their best judgments on the more difficult and complex issues.

Where do we get our candidates for public office?

Some individuals offer themselves for office through a sense of public service; others are impelled by personal ambition. Some are pushed into a candidacy by a partisan organization; others are put forth by special interest factions that want "their man" in government.

Few candidates are truly drafted by their peers. The "spontaneous draft" is usually a carefully planned and adroitly managed maneuver.

The Candidate Selection Process

How do you go about finding and choosing a candidate?

There are several routes. It depends on the political situation in your area and the amount of time you and your friends are willing to put into the task.

Quite often candidates are chosen by a selection (or, screening) committee. This is often the case where there is no incumbent running for re-election and a seat is wide open.

Sometimes the official party organization—or an unofficial partisan group—will from a *candidate selection committee,* screen the prospects, and endorse one individual. Sometimes an independent citizens committee will form an *ad hoc* group and get in on the selection act. And, quite often a special interest group (such as farmers, businessmen, environmentalists, organized labor, etc.) will form a *candidate search committee*—either on its own or in concert with compatible special interest groups.

You and your friends can become involved with one or more of those groups and try to influence their candidate selections. Or, you can conduct your own search, evaluate the contenders, and choose your own candidate from the field.

That decision will depend, in part, on whether any of the candidates selected by the various committees are acceptable to you. Whether they come close to representing your political philosophy. Whether they measure up to the moral and ethical standards you have set. Whether you feel one of the candidates is capable and qualified to represent you.

If any or all of the answers to those considerations are negative, you have these options:

—you can accept "the lesser of the evils" and support the "best" candidate

—you can sit it out (or work in another campaign), or

—you can field a candidate of your own choosing.

For the sake of delving more deeply into the candidate selection process, let's suppose that you and your friends decide to find the man or woman of your own choice.

The Search for a Candidate

Remember the folks who got involved with you in that first venture into government and politics? The neighbors and friends who took the six-weeks course, *"In The Spirit of '76"?* And, the like-minded citizens in the town down the road who also took the course?

Call up those friends and neighbors and like-minded folks and invite them to the house for a cup of coffee and a little chat.

When they are assembled, remind them that they have been exceedingly unhappy with the incumbent, what's-his-name. Or, advise them that the congressional seat in the district will be up for grabs this time around; the incumbent is retiring, or running for the senate, or whatever.

Put it to them this way:

"Here is a great opportunity. Isn't it about time we had someone in that office who is God-centered, who practices the Christian ethic? Isn't it time we had someone truly concerned with the needs of the area? You bet it is!

"Let's get someone to run for the office. Let's get behind him and get him elected! Who shall it be?"

Urge the members of the group to make some suggestions, to come up with some names. It may be that you, or several folks in the group, already have one or two individuals in mind. Throw their names on the table. Get the others to do the same. Before the evening is over you will have come up with several good, solid prospects: capable, attractive, God-centered, winsome individuals.

If possible, your potential candidates should have a record of public service. Perhaps as a member of a school board, or the city council, or a local commission. Perhaps as a leader in community affairs such as the Salvation Army or a taxpayer's group. Perhaps as a prominent and successful business or professional leader who has devoted time to civic activities. Anything like that helps; it gives the candidate some name recognition with the voters and provides a better "poll position."

However, the individual who has no prior political track record but who scores high in other ways should not be overlooked. The voters are always interested in a bright, fresh—and clean—face.

The Attributes of a Good Candidate

What are the attributes you should seek when selecting the individual to be your candidate for public office?

First things first. Is the individual Christ-centered or is he self-centered? It's not a matter of wearing his religion on his sleeve, or his lapel; it's a matter of living the Christian faith.

God first. Then what?

Here are the six "C's" of a good candidate:

—*Clean* (Does the individual have any skeletons rattling around in his private or public closet? Anything to be ashamed of? Anything that could flare up and cause voter disgust or doubt? In a political campaign you can be sure "Your sins will find you out".)

—*Clear* (Is the individual articulate? Does he make sense? Can he express himself clearly and forcefully? Is he willing and able to say what he means and do it in a convincing and positive manner? Can he get to the nub of an issue and discuss it cogently?)

—*Capable* (Does the individual have obvious abilities based on a record of success in private or public life? Has the individual done an outstanding job in some capacity? As chairman of some community effort, as leader in youth work, as a front-runner in his profession or industry?)

—*Constructive* (Does the individual have positive solutions to offer or is he simply a carping critic? Does he offer constructive alternatives? Sound ideas? Does he give reason to believe he can do a better job in office than the other fellow?)

—*Consistent* (Not bull-headed but steady. Not wishy-washy, not obnoxious, but firm. Or, does he jump from side to side in an effort to curry favor and win votes.)

—*Courageous* (Is the individual willing to take a stand and speak out on the issues? Even when the ground is rough and the going gets tough? Is he a leader, a person who inspires others to follow; one in whom the voters will have confidence? Does he convey the image that he will be a fighter for the best interests of his constituents and for the principles in which he believes?)

And, let's add a seventh "C"—*Conservative*. Is the potential candidate a staunch supporter of individual liberty, constitutional government, competitive free enterprise, fiscal responsibility and morality in office?

Those are all things the voter looks for in sizing up a candidate and deciding on his vote. *The smart selection committee will look for them too—first;* before they pledge themselves to a candidate and his campaign.*

Good Health and Stamina

One more thing: the candidate you select should be in good health and have plenty of stamina to stand the rigors of campaigning.

The odds are that the candidate you select will not be a wealthy person and you know he will not be backed by a high-powered and well-financed machine. Besides, "buying" elections is not what good citizenship is all about. Thus, the candidate will have to get out and "sell" himself, or herself, to the voters. Part of that sales job will include meeting the voters (as many as possible), talking to them, winning their support and their votes. *That takes lots of time and lots of work; it takes energy and endurance.*

Be sure your candidate understands, at the outset, that campaigning for public office can be a grueling experience. *Make sure your candidate is a hard worker.* Lazy candidates seldom win elections.

Make a Checklist

With those, and any other, desirable traits in mind make up a score card—a checklist. Ask each one in your group to "grade"

---

* Ray C. Bliss, for many years the Republican chairman in Ohio, once offered these as the qualities of a good candidate, based on a voter survey: concern for the problems of people, honesty, leadership, experience in government, free of political party ties, reliability and trustworthiness, good education, good financial and business background, and young (not necessarily in age, but in spirit).

the individuals being considered as a potential candidate. Tally
the totals. How do they stack up? Does one of the potential candidates meet the criteria you set forth? If not, keep looking. It
is better to take the time for a thorough search than to settle on
"almost" and regret it later.

This initial phase of candidate selection may take more than
one meeting. If so, at your next meeting why not expand the circle?
Invite like-minded friends from the neighboring tract, or the nearby
town.

When you have agreed on a person who meets your requirements,
you are ready for the next step. Sure it's work. But finding the
right individual to represent you in government is important business. If you let George do it, chances are George will be represented
and you may not be.

Candidate Questionnaire

Now is the time to make up a candidate questionnaire.

List the important public issues. Those of real concern to the
members of your group and to the citizens of the district. Make
sure the list includes only those issues that will be handled at the
level of government in which your candidate may serve. After all,
a state legislator would hardly get involved in maintaining posses-
sion of the Panama Canal or improving the postal service.

Don't load the questionnaire. *Make it straight.* That way you
are more likely to get straight answers and the kind of sound
information that can help you and your friends get an accurate
picture of where the potential candidate stands, what he really
believes, and where his philosophy lies. It will also give you an
indication as to whether he can and does apply his basic beliefs
to contemporary issues and answers.

Interviewing the Candidate

It's now time to check formally with the prospective candidate,
or candidates.

Assign two or three members of the group the chore of contacting each of the individuals on your potential candidate list (those who earned high marks on those tally sheets). The job of the interview-team is (a.) to find out if the individual is interested and willing to run for office and, if so, (b). to go through the candidate questionnaire with him or her. (Incidentally, don't take the first "No, not interested" as the final answer from the potential candidate; reluctance to run for office is not a bad initial reaction.)

After the interview team or teams report back to the group, and their findings have been discussed and evaluated, invite the acceptable candidate to a meeting of the entire membership. Let the other members meet the man or woman, and ask questions. *Don't shy away from the hard questions.* It's better to probe now than to have the opposition dig up something unexpected and damaging late in the campaign.

Through this, or a similar screening and selection process, you can find the right candidate. And, when the candidate says "Yes" and your group says "Yes", you're on your way.

Do you think all this is an over-simplification or an exaggeration of how a candidate is selected? It isn't. There are many officeholders in the federal congress and the state legislatures and local school boards who were first elected to that office because two or three or maybe a dozen citizens got together and searched and screened and stewed and finally decided "that's the one!"

Then they went to work—and elected him, or her!

CHAPTER SIX

The Building Of A Candidate

"If, to please the people, we offer what we ourselves disapprove,
how can we afterward defend our work?"
George Washington

Now that your committee has found the best man or woman for the office—federal, state or local—the job is to "sell" the candidate to the voters—or, at least to a majority of those who go to the polls come election day.

A Marketing Program

Let's set up a basic marketing plan to present our candidate to the voters in the district. This plan can be expanded or condensed, depending upon the nature of the campaign and the scope of the election. However, it is best to consider a basic plan because in that way you will know better what to add, or delete.

First, the candidate (in the most constructive sense, "the product").

What kind of a person is he, or she? If the screening and selection group did its job well, you have as a candidate an individual who has some outstanding attributes that should be attractive to a large number of voters. Those "Eight Cs", for example:

Christ-centered, clean, clear, capable, constructive, consistent, courageous, and conservative.*

Second, the candidate's record of achievement and service in public affairs—if not in politics and government, in other areas of endeavor. List those accomplishments, concisely and attractively. Include any civic or service or special awards for outstanding achievement. List his, or her, memberships and past or present offices in service, civic, community, professional, church, military and other patriotic organizations (each one of those groups has a following).

Put these vital data on a sheet of paper, along with a short resume of the candidate's personal background (age, marital status, number of children, education, present occupation, etc.). Put it in a file folder along with several good photographs (head shots) of the candidate. You will use that information again and again, in the coming months and when the "formal" campaign gets under-way.

A word about those pictures of the candidate:

Avoid the arty and the studio portrait. Capture the natural image of the candidate. Portray the kind of candidate you will be present-ing to the voter: if one of the attributes is youth and vitality, have a file on that type of picture. If the image is maturity, wisdom, thoughtfulness—capture that in the photograph. Above all, have the candidate look the camera (the voter) square in the eye; pleasant but open and direct. If the theme of the campaign is to be "ac-tion"—"He gets things done"—the photographs should show the

---

* An August, 1974, public opinion poll done for TIME magazine by Yankelovich, Skelly & White, Inc., "confirmed the wide-spread belief" that most Americans are moving toward the right. A total of 51% of those interviewed in the poll indicated they were conservative or leaning conserv-ative. The Gallup Poll of May, 1974, indicated 59 percent considered themselves conservative.

candidate at work, busy, getting things done; not posed "make-work" but honest-to-goodness work.

Third, consider the candidate's personality. In what type of a setting does he, or she, really shine forth?

Is it before large audiences, or small groups? Is the candidate a better-than-average speaker? Dynamic on the platform? Or, better in the give-and-take of discussion groups, a member of a panel, a participant in talk shows, coffee hours and socials?

Dependent on the answer to those questions, you should *design the candidate's speaking schedule.* If the candidate is a good public speaker try to get appearances before the various service clubs, church groups, civic organizations, community meetings, etc. Most of those groups are always looking for a good speaker on a topic of interest; you should have no trouble in setting up a busy schedule—*one or two talks each week, if possible.*

If the candidate does best at smaller functions, then set up a number of neighborhood coffees, or receptions, small get-togethers, and work to get him or her included on panels and discussion groups before the local taxpayers association, or parent-teacher's meetings, etc. Use these smaller affairs to reach as many of the key opinion leaders and community heirarchy as you can. These contacts will be important as the campaign develops and the "formal" phase begins.

In all of these efforts, remember this:

Try to place the candidate in situations which employ his, or her, best abilities and attributes. That not only casts the candidate in the most favorable light, it makes the candidate more comfortable, and it builds more self-assurance. That adds up to a better presentation and a more positive impression on the minds of those with whom he, or she, comes in contact.

Accentuate The Positive

What is the candidate's chief area of expertise? What is that subject or field of endeavor in which he, or she, has had the most experience, knows the most about and can discuss most fluently?

Is it medicine? Medical economics, health care, drug-related problems—these are major issues in most communities these days. Is it education? There's an important issue! Is it some aspect of engineering or science? Those professions can be keys to solving some of the pressing problems such as pollution, conservation, the energy shortage, creation of new jobs. Is it industrial or commercial management? Jobs, and the creation of new jobs, and sound financial know-how are important to a healthy economy.

Whatever it is—agriculture, working with youth, knowledge of criminal law—*use that strength to good advantage*. Tie it, and the candidate, to the important issues of the area or district. Apply it, and the candidate, to items of importance and interest in the community. Develop the campaign theme or thrust around it. Base some of the candidate's major speeches and key literature on it. Keep pressing the fact that "here is a person who can—*who really can*—be of important service to us and to the community".

Take Care!

What about the "opposition"? The other party or the other candidate?

In the typical political campaign, the opposition is "the enemy" and anything goes—as long as you don't get caught. Things that are not quite ethical, or not quite truthful, are often excused with a smile and a shrug and "Oh, well. All's fair in love and war and politics. After all, we're in this to win, right?"

Wrong! All is not fair in love or war or politics and the desire to win cannot excuse bending the truth or breaking the Golden Rule. Bad means do not serve good ends; they do not serve The Lord and they do not serve the public.

Suppose you could win a close election by stretching a point or twisting the truth—just a fraction. Suppose you did and your candidate won. What have you won? You're probably right back where you started except that now the power of office is corrupting you instead of the other guy.

As for the public, it would be worse off than before. There *was* the hope that Christians would make a difference in politics, that they would restore morality to government. Even that hope would be gone. What kind of a witness would that be?

So, take care! Stand fast in your faith and strong in your ethics.

There are undoubtedly some honest differences of political philosophy, or proposed programs, between your candidate and his opponent; between "your" side and "their" side. Is it proper to point out those differences? To criticize the opposition's position and to state why your stand is the correct one? *Certainly!* Provided . . .

. . . *provided* that what is presented for comparison is the truth, the whole truth, and not a half-truth dressed up to mislead the public.

. . . *provided* that no material (no quote, no vote, no record or fact) is taken out of context to convey an incorrect impression.

. . . *and, provided* that no unwarranted assumptions are drawn and no unsubstantiated conclusions are suggested as fact.

Check the Scriptures. We are clearly admonished to have no part of any false witness, or deceit, or innuendo. *And nowhere does it say "except in politics" or, "this applies to all things but political campaigns".*

Smears Are A No-No!

Many professionals will contend that the winning campaign strategy must have two parts, a positive and a negative:

"You gotta promote your candidate, and you gotta tear down the opposition.

"People vote against someone, or something, as much as they vote for someone, or something. So, you gotta blast away at your opponent and make the people want to vote against him."

Well, Christians should have no part of that. None at all!

Even if that were the only way to win, who needs it? Where is the profit if a man gain the world (or win an election) and lose his soul?

So, concentrate on the positive. Shun the negative. Merchandise the merits and the abilities and the promises of your candidate;

let the opposition wage its own campaign.

Research your opponent's public record—his votes, his speeches, his public proposals, the bills he sponsored, or whatever. Study them. It will help your candidate sharpen his own views on those issues; it will help articulate the distinction between the two candidates, and it will enable you and your candidate to increase the integrity and appeal of his position on those issues. And that is all to the good.

But, don't waste your time looking under rocks or sticking your hand in the mud. That has no magic to stir men's souls; it offers no solutions to America's problems . . . and it violates the Golden Rule.

Issues and Targets

Stephen C. Shadegg, lay leader in the Episcopal church and a political practitioner of national renown, offers this advice on "reaching" people:

"If you want the voters to listen, you must say something of interest to them." *

First you must find out what is important to the voters you are trying to reach; then, you must talk to them about those issues and concerns. That's the way to get their attention and maintain their interest—*and that is one of the hardest jobs in any campaign.*

Gimmicks and gadgets and puffery and stunts may be more spectacular of the moment but a campaign based on constructive proposals, positive programs, and suggested solutions—*smartly and dynamically presented (packaged)*—will get more votes for the candidate and be of far greater service to the public. Especially if those proposals and programs and solutions are geared to the issues of greatest concern to the voters.

What are the issues, or issue-clusters, of real concern to the voters in the district?

(An issue-cluster is a group of distinct but related issues that, when properly combined, add up to a matter of major concern

---

* *"How to Win an Election"*, Stephen C. Shadegg, Taplinger, 1964

to a large number of voters. An example would be *the high cost of living.* The individual issues within that cluster would include heavy taxation, inflation (the shrinking dollar), the excessive cost and bureaucracy of government, high interest rates, etc.)

What are the major voter-blocs in your district that warrant special attention? Not necessarily ethnic blocs, or economic blocs, but *issue-blocs.* How do you reach them, on what issue, from what angle?

(For example, there may be a sizable Pro-Life/Anti-Abortion bloc in the district; individuals in all walks of society, all economic segments, all religious faiths, who strongly oppose pro-abortion laws. These citizens cut across all established "groupings"; their ranks are usually well-organized with good lines of communications; they are usually articulate and active. If the candidate believes in the right to life, this is certainly one of the blocs that should be lined up in his vote column—if he works to get it.)

But, how do you find out about these important issues, and these key voter blocs? Not by what you, or the candidate, or the committee think they are. Not by guess and by golly. Not by intuition. No sir!

You find out what's really bugging the citizens through motivational research. Don't let that term scare you; it's sort of a five-dollar label for a public opinion survey, or market research. And, it is essential to any campaign—*any campaign,* regardless of the level of the office being sought, or the size of the election district involved, or the amount of money in the campaign budget.

So, let's take a poll and find out about those issues and voter targets.

Public Opinion Polls

In a larger campaign—for a statewide office, or for a congressional district or the state legislature—research should be an important item in the budget. Some experts suggest that at least *ten percent* of the budget be used for polling.

A highly competent research group should be retained to do

the surveys. That's surveys, *plural;* surveys should be taken in waves, or in series, starting with the very early stages of the campaign and repeated periodically with the final installment taken during the closing weeks. That way you can keep track of the *tides and shifts* in public opinion and keep tabs on any *emerging issues.*

Remember this: the proper use of a poll in a campaign is not simply to see who's ahead in the race; the purpose of a poll—if it is to be of real value to the campaign—is to determine *what the issues are,* what the voters (and voter blocs) *feel* about the issues, *what they think should be done* about the issues and problems, and *what (if anything) the voters think about the competing candidates —and why.* Properly directed, properly used and analyzed, a poll can provide important *decision insurance* in the campaign; improperly designed and used, it is a waste of money, can instill a false sense of confidence (or frustration) and be an instrument for defeat rather than victory.

Smaller campaigns—those with limited funds, those for school board, or city council, or a county seat, in suburban or rural areas—usually cannot afford the services of a professional research organization. But, for them opinion research is still a must and there are two alternatives:

First, join with another compatible and non-competing candidate (or several others) to finance a public opinion survey on a *joint-basis.* That will at least provide some bench-marks and direction signals.

Second, you can conduct your own survey, using *volunteers.* Professional researchers will scoff at that suggestion. Granted a poll conducted by volunteers will not be as scientific or as precise in its findings but it *will* provide the campaign with some important information. And, in some cases, volunteer polls have come suprisingly close to the findings developed by the professional shop.

To repeat: whether you can afford a professional research organization, or whether you must rely on volunteers, make every effort to base your campaign strategy on voter opinion research. Do this not to compromise, but to strategize: *when you compromise, you change your principles; when you strategize, you change your tactics.* There is a *big* difference!

Quick Review

Okay! Let's step back for a moment and review some things. We have selected the candidate. We know his, or her, strong points and best qualities. We are going to arrange the candidate's meet-and-speak *schedule* to take advantage of those.

We have determined those areas, those fields, in which the candidate has solid experience and valuable (marketable) expertise. We are going to *design the campaign thrust* to make the strongest and most positive use of those assets.

We are preparing (or have started) our *market research* operations. We will find out what the important issues are, what's bugging the voters, and what the political climate is.

What's next? Well, it's U.V.P.!

The Unique Voter Proposition

That's right, U.V.P. *The Unique Voter Proposition.*
Its forebearer was U.S.P., the Unique Sales Proposition. U.S.P. has sparked some of the most successful advertising and sales campaigns in America.* Since its inception some 30 years ago, U.S.P. has been imitated, altered, used and mis-used. Those advertisers who have used it thoughtfully, correctly and honestly have had some amazing results.

The basics, and the power, of U.S.P. can be effectively employed in the winning political campaign.

These are *the essentials* of a Unique Voter Proposition:

—it is *a specific and direct proposition* to the voter. It is not a gimmick, or an unwarranted boast, or a slick promise.

—it is *designed to be unique* (the sole "property" of your candidate and one that his opposition cannot duplicate).

—it is a *clear and compelling* gesture that will move the voter to your candidate.

---

* *"Reality in Advertising"*, Rosser Reeves, Alfred A. Knopf, 1961

Do not confuse U.V.P. with what the political "pro" calls the campaign "theme". General Dwight Eisenhower's 1952 "I will go to Korea" was a Unique Voter Proposition.

It involved an *issue of burning voter concern* (people wanted that war ended); it was *a specific commitment* ("I will go . . ."); it was *clear* (no ifs, ands or buts, "I will go to Korea."). And it was *unique* (as the former General of the Armies, the proposition was Ike's, and only Ike's. Adlai Stevenson could not imitate it, or steal it, or weaken it.).

John F. Kennedy's 1960 call for a "New Frontier" was *not* a U.V.P. It was more of a *campaign theme*. Attractive but not unique; catchy but not concise. It did not lock onto any specific issue (although it touched on several) and it could be imitated and parroted—and was.

A Unique Voter Proposition, once made, can be *used and re-used in all facets of the campaign*—speeches, advertising, literature, precinct work, etc. The difference between a theme and a U.V.P. is the difference between a trademark and a bugle call; between the sound of rain and a clap of thunder.

Here's an illustration of how U.V.P. might be applied even in a *local* election contest against the incumbent mayor.

If the challenger promises the voters that he will fight crime, that's a *ho-hum* deal. It is not a U.V.P.; what candidate won't "fight crime"? But, if he announces that "if elected I will fire the Chief of Police!", that is indeed a U.V.P. It promises the voter *a specific benefit* to be realized *if* they vote for the candidate. And, it is especially a U.V.P. if the incumbent mayor is one of the chief's cronies and belongs to the same political machine!

You cannot develop a truly stunning U.V.P. without first doing your public opinion research (the polls told Eisenhower's campaign managers that Korea was the major issue at that time). Many campaigns spend thousands of dollars on research and never come up with anything close to a Unique Voter Proposition; in some of them, U.V.P. could spell the difference between victory and defeat.

CHAPTER SEVEN

The Extra-Early Start

"A political campaign is a bit like an iceberg. The average citizen sees only the tip, the part that shows. But underneath there is a structure that has been built through long hours and days and months—and even years—of planning and work and worry and volunteers."

Tom R. Van Sickle
National Chairman,
Young Republicans, 1965-67

Most manuals on politics deal almost exclusively with the obvious, or traditional, parts of the political campaign.*

There is, or should be, another phase of a well-planned and
well-run campaign: *the extra-early or preparatory phase.*

This extra-early phase begins as soon as you have found your
candidate. (Actually, it can begin even while you are selecting the
candidate.) It extends from then through the day when your candidate publicly announces his, or her candidacy. It includes those
months of quiet planning, low-level effort and trial-and-error preparation that will enable you to kick off your "official campaign"

---

*The official (public) campaign starts shortly before the candidate an-
nounces and extends, with increased momentum, through election day.

with a flying start and with most of your committees in high gear.

Here are a few of the benefits the extra-early period can provide for your committee and your candidate:

—give the committee time for the *preliminary building* of the candidate

—give the candidate (and committee) time to make those all-important advance *contacts with key opinion leaders* in the community

—provide lead-time in which to *develop, test and strengthen* some of the main parts of the campaign organization

—give you time to *develop, market-test and revise or tighten* the candidate's position and presentation in regard to basic issues

—enable you early-on to *locate, recruit, and train* key personnel for both the headquarters and field forces

—allow you to *stockpile ideas, issue-ammunition, and plans* for subsequent special events and projects

—create an *air of expectancy* and an *earlier interest* in your candidate, and

—make it easier for your fund-raisers to *accumulate a good portion of the money* that will be needed for the full-blown campaign (you should always start the campaign with "money in the bank").

NOW Is None Too Soon!

Hopefully, you completed your candidate screening and selection long before election day. Ideally it should have been done one year or more before the voters go to the polls.

You will need all the time you can get to place your candidate's name before the public; all the time you can get to publicize his, or her, positive qualities; all the time you can get to make widely-known the candidate's position on important issues and solutions to pressing problems.

Incumbents vs. Newcomers

If your candidate is a "fresh face"—a newcomer to politics—you will need the extra-early start and the added time it provides.

An incumbent is generally considered to have the edge over the challenger in any bid for re-election. Some experts figure that incumbency is worth five to seven percentage points when projecting the votes in a contest between an incumbent and a challenger.

This edge may have diminished during recent times, because of the public's attitude toward politicians and officeholders. But, figure that the incumbent has the edge going in; use that to inspire your candidate and committee to work harder—*and longer.*

Remember: incumbency is an "edge" but it is not the victory!

A Couple Of Hurdles

Even without an incumbent in the race, the newcomer must overcome some built-in disadvantages.

First, there is the problem of *name recognition* and identification. "Who's this fella Joe Smith? The guy who's running for . . . what's he running for, anyway? How come he thinks he's qualified to represent me? What's he ever done?"

Second, there is the job of making known the *candidate's position on the important issues.* "Where does he stand on farm subsidies? What's he going to do to fight the high cost of living?" And, "What is he, a liberal or a conservative?"

The candidate's stand on the important issues is of real interest to people who care enough to vote and can be influential in attracting citizens *who might not ordinarily vote.* And, the candidate's political philosophy and identification is of special concern to active party members.

Recognize these hurdles for what they are—as being real but *certainly not insurmountable.* Not if your committee and your candidate get to work!

Starting The Team

Chapter Eight *("Building The Winning Team")* deals with the structure of the campaign committee and discusses the authority

and responsibilities of the various chairmen and their subcommittees. Although many of the suggestions made in that chapter apply
to the "formal" campaign, some of those pointers apply equally
to the extra-early phases.

Now, for example, is the time to select a general chairman. And,
a co-chairman. It is necessary to have a focal point of authority
and decision to keep things moving—and moving on time and on
target. (Read the sections on *"General Chairman"* and *"Co-Chairman"* in Chapter Eight, and make them your guide in considering
the abilities and experience you should look for in the persons
you appoint to those two top spots in the campaign. Obviously,
the candidate should have final approval on these selections before
the appointments are made, since he must work closely and constantly with both chairmen.)

Following the selection of the chairman and co-chairman, four
key subcommittee chairmen should be appointed and their committees put into operation:

—*Scheduling*
—*Research & Analysis*
—*Publicity,* and
—*Finance.*

Again, the general duties of these chairmen and their committees
are outlined in Chapter Eight. At this point, let's consider some
of their functions in the *extra-early phase* of the campaign.

Scheduling

The functions of the scheduling committee fall into three categories:

1. *to help obtain and schedule the candidate's public appearances
and speaking engagements*

2. *to coordinate the candidate's speaking schedule and to keep
the candidate and campaign chairman fully advised on the pertinent
details of those scheduled appearances,* and

3. *to monitor the candidate's appearances for audience reaction,
impact, and feedback.*

The Scheduling Chairman should work with the other committee members and outside contacts to obtain candidate appearances before as many worthwhile and diverse groups as possible. It is part of the task of the scheduling operations to make sure that those appearances make the *best possible use* of the candidate's time (size of group, importance of its membership, etc.).

It is also the job of the scheduling chairman to make sure that these engagements are carefully coordinated so that there are no conflicts in times or dates that might embarrass the candidate. If this operation is sloppy, and the candidate is accidentally scheduled before two groups at the same time and has to cancel or miss one of these appointments, that will cost you—*in lost votes.*

All—*repeat, all*—of the candidate's public appearances should be channeled through the scheduling committee. There is a "bonus" to this rule: it will often enable the candidate, or the campaign chairman, to avoid or escape a sticky situation by simply telling the person pressing for a date that "I'll have to check with our scheduling people to make sure there is no conflict on that day (or, at that time)."

Coffee In The Precincts

Make this a goal: a neighborhood coffee klatch for the candidate in every precinct in your district. Start these now, during the extra-early period, and make sure the candidate attends every one.

Granted, this can make for a grueling schedule for the candidate and a great deal of work for the precinct captains—*but it will be worth it!*

In these days of cynicism and suspicion about politics and politicians it is important that the voters have an opportunity to meet your candidate and see for themselves that he is "really something else". . . . that he is warm and human, honest and forthright, and "one of us".

If time and organization does not permit one coffee in every precinct, then be sure—be sure—to have a candidate's coffee *in every one of your priority precincts.* And, do this as far ahead of election day as possible. Schedule several each day. Start out by asking the ladies in your study group to hold coffees in their precincts, and then build from there.

The benefits of these coffees should be obvious:

—they provide the candidate with the opportunity *to meet as many voters as possible* (at least 10 to 20 at each coffee)

—they provide voters the opportunity *to meet the candidate firsthand* and hear his, or her, political views and positions on the issues—plus permitting the voters to ask questions on the issues that concern them

—they provide precinct captains with the opportunity *to invite prospective blockworkers* to these coffees to meet the candidate and also give the precinct captains the chance to line up additional recruits, and

—they help build the *candidate's name recognition* (and goodwill) in advance of voter canvassing by the blockworkers.

At these precinct coffees, the candidate should tell something of his, or her, background, experience and political philosophy, discuss one or two important issues, and *ask for questions* from the audience. Keep the atmosphere warm, friendly and informal. Assure the coffee hostess that all that is expected is coffee and/or tea and a few cookies.

Volunteer sign-up cards (for precinct workers, headquarters help, bumper stickers and lawn cards, etc.) should be available; also, a neatly printed but not expensive piece of literature setting forth the candidate's background, views on the issues, and outstanding qualities. Do not ask for campaign contributions at this first coffee. If someone should volunteer a contribution, or a pledge, accept it with gratitude. *But, the real purpose of these precinct coffees is to get votes for your candidate and workers for his campaign.*

And remember: be sure to follow up on those volunteer sign-up cards. Don't lose a willing worker!

Trial Runs

Unless you are sure that the candidate is a polished speaker—accustomed to addressing strange groups—schedule some trial runs.

VOLUNTEER SIGN-UP CARD

Date _____ Block # _____ Precinct # _____	(Space above this line for headquarters use)

YOU BET! I want to help elect _____ (candidate's name)
to _____ (office).

_____

NAME   (Last)   (First)

_____

ADDRESS   (Phone number)

YOU CAN COUNT ON ME TO:

( ) Be a blockworker for _____ (candidate's name)

( ) Distribute candidate's literature

( ) Help at campaign headquarters

( ) Work at home (help with mailings, etc.)

( ) Have a coffee for the candidate

( ) Work on election day

( ) Contribute $_____ by ___ (date) ___ or   ( ) $_____
     each month, _____ to _____

( ) Other _____

Print enough of these sign-up cards to have a sufficient supply for all coffees and other meetings and for headquarters use— plus a quantity for hand-out purposes. If you can afford to have these cards printed, fine. If not, mimeograph the text on 4″ x 6″ file cards.

Set up his first public appearances before *relatively small and obscure* groups. If his first time out is a "bomb", the damage will be minimal; he can rewrite his remarks and practice his style and delivery before the next appearance.

It may take several of these trial runs before his delivery and messages are polished—and the candidate feels "ready". That's when scheduling can begin to place him before the larger and more important meetings.

Detail Sheets & Confirmation Forms

The scheduling chairman should prepare a *detail sheet* to be used whenever a public appearance is obtained for the candidate. This detail sheet should provide the candidate, and the campaign chairman, with the pertinent details of the engagement—*where, when, who, what, etc.*

This detail sheet should be made out *in triplicate:* one copy for the candidate, one for the campaign chairman, and one for the scheduling chairman's master file.

Scheduling should also prepare and have reproduced sufficient copies of a "confirmation" form to be used for each and every engagement on behalf of the candidate.

This confirmation sheet should be sent to the chairman, or program chairman, of the group before which the candidate has agreed to appear. It should be sent as soon as possible after accepting a speaking engagement so that there is no doubt in anyone's mind that the candidate will be there.

Along with that confirmation, the scheduling chairman should send a copy of the *candidate's background sheet* (or biography) or—better yet—a sheet of *suggested introductory remarks.* (Those introductory remarks are a minor but important detail: they will save the program chairman of the meeting time and worry, and they will help make sure that the introduction contains the points the candidate, or the campaign chairman, wants made.)

Sample copies of both the "Scheduling Detail Sheet" and the "Confirmation Form" are included in The Appendix.

Feedback

The third important function of the scheduling committee is to *monitor the candidate's public appearances* and to provide the candidate and the campaign chairman with "feedback" on audience reaction; how the candidate did, the weak and strong points in his presentation (delivery and speech content), comments from individuals in the audience, and—in general—the level of acceptance, agreement and/or disagreement evidenced by those in attendance.

This can be done by assigning a member of the scheduling committee (or a member of one of the other campaign subcommittees) to accompany the candidate to each meeting. Or, it may be possible to arrange for one of the friendly individuals in the audience to do the chore for the committee. Whichever, *monitoring is important.* It helps the candidate improve his presentation and it helps the committee make sure the candidate's message is hitting home and getting public acceptance.

Never Alone

The candidate should never travel alone or be asked to travel alone. A friend, or neighbor, or committee member should always accompany him to these appearances. This includes even those times when the candidate's spouse is along.

Why? Because:

1. *it creates a better impression* (the candidate who arrives alone and unknown at a strange meeting place often conveys the image of a "nobody" going "nowhere")

2. *it saves wear and tear on the candidate* (the friend or companion can do the driving—so that the candidate can think about the forth-coming appearance, go over his notes or text, or shut his eyes and relax and meditate for a few minutes)

3. *it can prevent embarrassing and time-consuming incidents* (the person accompanying the candidate can help extricate him, or her, from prolonged discussions with "talkers" by courteously and pleasantly saying to the candidate, "I'm sorry to have to break this up, but we must leave now to make your next appointment." This may not be so important in the early-on stages of the campaign but toward the closing days, when time is really of the essence, this will be vital.).

Publicity

A dynamic publicity program is one of the key facets of any successful campaign. Even during the extra-early phase, there should be a well-planned and executed effort to get the name, picture and activities of the candidate-to-be before the public.

Appoint a competent individual as *Publicity Chairman.* Do this right at the start of the extra-early period.

Because of the importance of this job, the publicity chairman should be a person who can put *a great deal of time and effort* into the work. If the campaign can afford to employ a professional publicist, on either a full or part-time basis, *great!* Do it! If not, here are some suggestions for your search for a volunteer publicity chairman:

—*a friendly local newsman, or woman (or advertising executive)* who is on your side and wants to help

—a person working in the *publicity department* of a local company, union or community organization

—*a retired person* who has had either professional or extensive volunteer publicity experience, or

—*a college student* (perhaps a graduate student in journalism or political science) who likes the candidate-to-be and agrees with what he stands for. What this young person might lack in experience and know-how he, or she, could well make up in energy, dedication and fresh ideas.

In addition to helping *build public awareness* of the candidate-to-be during the extra-early stage, the publicity chairman can use the time to:

—*prepare campaign materials* such as the candidate's official biography (for future use in press kits, mailouts, speech introductions, etc.)

—*draft "one-pagers"* on the candidate's position *on key issues* (for future distribution to campaign workers, opinion leaders, mail queries, etc.)

—draft the copy for planned *campaign literature* (flyers, brochures, handout cards, issue pamphlets, etc.)

—build a *list of the area media* (all media—newspapers, radio,

TV, special trade and professional publications, organization news bulletins, in-house (company and union) magazines, etc.)
  —start cultivating the *key people on those media* (to build or strengthen acquaintances), and
  —*assist the scheduling chairman* in obtaining speaking engagements for the candidate-to-be and servicing the various contacts involved with publicity and background material, etc.

A Suggestion

In the extra-early stages, publicity material should probably *not* mention that "(name) is (or, will be) a candidate for (office)". Hold off on that for a while.

Base the publicity releases on the fact that he, or she, is a "leading spokesman in the fight for (whatever)" or "one of the prime movers in the Citizens Committee for Lower Taxes (or, whatever)" or "president of Acme Foundry" or "former president of the Elk Grove PTA and prominent in the drive to obtain released time for religious education for local school students", etc.

This is not deceit. It is a matter of careful timing; holding off on any official announcement of candidacy until the most opportune moment. Of course, if someone (a newsman, for example) should ask, be totally open and honest: "Yes, a group of us citizens are working for (name)'s candidacy and he has given his approval. There's nothing secret about it; we're just trying to get our organization (or, effort) lined up before we make a public announcement."

Research Committee

Good research is vital to the winning campaign. It can help furnish the issue-ammunition and direct the deployment of the precinct workers—two extremely important operations in the election effort.

A *Research Chairman* should be appointed at the outset of the extra-early phase of the campaign. The capabilities and duties of this chairman are outlined in Chapter Eight. Because of the importance of this work, and the heavy work load during certain periods of the campaign, it is wise to appoint a Research Co-chairman to help with the job.

The research committee provides these important services, among others:

1. *gathers and builds the campaign research files* (including background materials and factual data on the key issues, factual information on the opposition, and statistical data and analysis on the political climate of the district)

2. *assists in the public opinion polls* (whether these are done by a professional organization or by volunteers), and

3. *makes a statistical analysis of the voting habits of the district*

The important attributes of the research chairman, and those who work on this committee, are accuracy, thoroughness, and speed. A serious public mis-statement by the candidate—based on inaccurate information from the research chairman—can be severely damaging, sometimes fatal, to the campaign.

Public Opinion Polls

The importance of opinion polls has already been stressed in Chapter Six. Campaigns that cannot afford the services of a professional research organization, should do some polling through the use of volunteers.

College students and housewives can do this job, and do it well. Quite often a marketing or social science class can be persuaded to take on the survey as a class project. Sometimes, in return, you may be asked to make a small gift to the school fund, or to pay a small hourly fee to the students.

Many housewives, especially those who are out-going and pleasant and direct, make good interviewers.

Volunteer pollsters must keep in mind that they are to be *totally objective;* their personal opinions must not be reflected—either in the way they ask the questions or in the way they respond to the answers to those questions. The best polling can be done *door-to-*

door, at random-selected houses. This permits the pollster to use issue cards (cards on which a set of issues are printed and from which the respondent can select those issues of prime importance to him), etc. However, if time and staff will not permit doorstep interviewing, the *polling can be done by phone* and the results obtained will probably be within an acceptable margin of error.

There are three important points to keep in mind regarding these polls:

—the poll will be only as good as the *questionnaire* devised

—the *proper analysis* (interpretation) of the findings is critical, and

—ideally, for best results, there should be *at least three soundings* (surveys) made during the campaign—one six months before primary election day, one 60 days before primary, and the final one between the primary and the general election. And, if possible, the same respondents should be interviewed each time (in each of the three surveys). This is important if you are to correctly detect and measure any shifts in public opinion.

Even though you may use volunteer help to conduct the interviews, try to enlist *professional assistance* in setting up your sampling procedure, drawing up the questionnaires, and analyzing the results.

Statistical Analysis

The public opinion survey is taken to find out what the issues really are. Statistical analysis is done to find out *where the candidate's "votes" are*—in what precincts.

Statistical analysis of the district will target those precincts in which the candidate has the best opportunity to gain votes; to determine, in other words, your *priority hunting grounds.*

Some professional campaign managers call this "hunting where the ducks are".

There are few, if any, campaigns in which the organization can cover every single precinct in the election area. Thus, it is essential that you know where you should concentrate your precinct efforts—where you should deploy your precinct workers—*to make the most of the manpower and womanpower available.*

The technique for determining these priority (target) precincts is explained in *"The A-B-Cs of Statistical Analysis",* a special section in The Appendix. Since this statistical analysis involves the precincts, and since there will be a need for quite a few volunteers to assist in the clerical work involved, the research chairman should enlist the help of the precinct chairman for this operation.

In Summary

Remember this: all of the activities outlined in this chapter—the early-on organizational work, the public appearances, the neighborhood coffees, the initial publicity and the first-phases of the research work—all of this *can and should be well along before* the candidate makes the big announcement and the campaign begins in earnest.

Once that official declaration of candidacy is made, it will be more difficult to get speaking dates before nonpolitical groups; it will be more difficult to get a steady stream of publicity in the media . . . and the materials and survey findings and statistical analyses of the district will be needed, *like right away!*

So, *make the extra-early start time count!* It's building a foundation for the subsequent campaign structure.

CHAPTER EIGHT

Building The Winning Team

> "There is no substitute for the local organization and there is no substitute for doorbell-ringing and shoe leather. If you want to win an election—national, state or local—you still have to reach the individual voter through your local worker."
>
> *Leonard W. Hall*
> *Republican National Chairman,*
> *1953-57*

There are four essentials to a winning campaign:
—a good *candidate*
—strong *issues*
—enough *money,* and
—a good *campaign organization.*

The fact is that even with a mediocre candidate and luke-warm issues and a minimal amount of money, a good campaign organization can win elections. The old-time—and some not so old-time—political machines serve as evidence, if not example.

Fortunately, you have a good candidate. Issues prompted you and your associates to get involved. And, quite often the question of sufficient campaign funds is directly related to the type of organization you have. So, let's look into the makings of a strong campaign organization—let's consider *how to build a winning team.*

Geared To Sales

Building a campaign organization to elect a candidate has a lot in common with putting together a sales or marketing operation:

You are creating an apparatus to "sell" your candidate to the voters. Not that the candidate is a bar of soap, or a can of beans; and, not that you want to bamboozle the public with a toothpaste smile or a shock of hair. There has been too much of that already. What we need now is less "style" and more substance.

With the right candidate, you can sell substance—ability, integrity, morality, brains, and the willingness to serve the people. Your "product" is an individual who believes that holding public office is a sacred trust; akin to the priesthood.

You believe your candidate is like that; you know he, or she, has those important attributes. But, the voters do not. The purpose of your campaign organization is to see that they do by the time election day rolls around.

Don't Over-Organize!

The political parties may have their difference in philosophy but on one thing they agree: *organization is most often the secret of success.*

The campaign that fails to organize usually ends up like the guy in the cartoon: his desk piled high with unattended work, the floor littered with important notes, and he's on the phone saying *"Next week we've gotta get organized."* BUT, next week is the election!

However, take care. *Don't over-organize.* The campaign that is overly-structured is not a good one. It ends up using most of its energy and resources to operate itself instead of the campaign. It becomes a "little federal government"; so busy with its own paperwork and red tape that it cannot perform the important campaign details.

What is presented here is a full-scale organization; the type of structure that might be used in a congressional or legislative, or even statewide, race. If your committee is going after a seat on the school board or the city council, it obviously will want a smaller, less structured organization. *So, build to fit the size of your campaign and work load.*

The base of the organizational pyramid is the most important part; and, that is the precinct organization. But, let's start at the top.

The Campaign Chairman

The campaign chairman is the ram-rod; the individual who makes it all happen and keeps it all together, moving in the right direction—and, *on schedule.*

The candidate who tries to be both general campaign chairman *and* a candidate is headed for trouble; *he cannot be both.* The candidate must be out front, meeting the public, making speeches, making news, reaching the voters; the chairman is in the back, *running the campaign.*

The most important qualification in a good campaign chairman is *executive ability:*

The ability to work well with people, and to get people to work together. *And, the ability to make decisions.* The chairman must lead, as a general leads his troops. *An indecisive chairman is a disaster.*

The chairman should be well and widely known in the election district. Preferably he should have had prior campaign experience. If the campaign can afford a *professional manager,* the fact that the chairman is not completely familiar with campaigning can be overlooked.

The chairman must have *a sense of priorities,* a sense of balance, *and a sense of timing.* He should have a concept and a grasp of all facets of the operation and an understanding of the duties of the various committees and chairmen who will be serving with him.

Generally the chairman is one of the *first appointments* made and should be appointed *during the extra-early phase* of the cam-

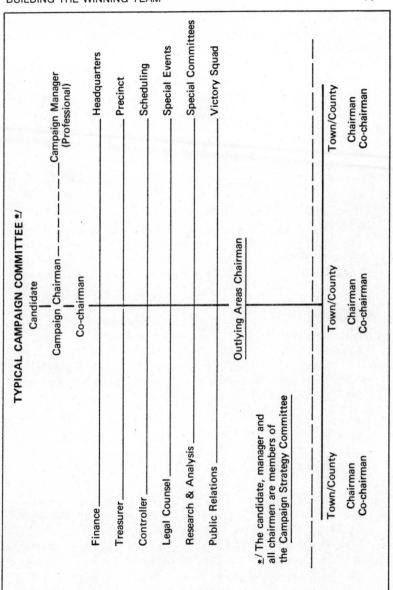

TYPICAL CAMPAIGN COMMITTEE */

Candidate

Campaign Chairman — — — — — Campaign Manager
(Professional)

Co-chairman

Finance ———————— Headquarters

Treasurer ———————— Precinct

Controller ———————— Scheduling

Legal Counsel ———————— Special Events

Research & Analysis ———————— Special Committees

Public Relations ———————— Victory Squad

Outlying Areas Chairman

Town/County   Town/County   Town/County   Town/County

Chairman   Chairman   Chairman   Chairman
Co-chairman   Co-chairman   Co-chairman   Co-chairman

*/ The candidate, manager and
all chairmen are members of
the Campaign Strategy Committee

paign so that he can be in on all the initial planning and strategy. From that point on, and in concert with the candidate, the chairman appoints the chairmen of the various subcommittees.

The chairmen of those subcommittees (detailed later in this chapter), plus the candidate, the campaign chairman (and the campaign manager if you employ one) comprise the *campaign strategy (or, steering) committee*. To see how this all fits together, refer to the chart ("Typical Campaign Committee") on page 75.

Campaign Co-Chairman

If the chairman is a man, *the co-chairman should be a woman,* and vice-versa. It is important to have a woman in the top ranks of the campaign—not only for her *"woman's view"* of the campaign (at least fifty percent of the voters are women) but also because at least one-half and probably more of the campaign workers will be women.

If the situation dictates a chairman who is a "figure head"—and that is inadvisable—make sure the co-chairman has all of the qualifications and experience required of the chairman.

The co-chairman generally *coordinates the activities of the various subcommittees.* That leaves the chairman free to work closely with the candidate (and the campaign manager) and to concentrate on planning, strategy, timing and fund-raising (in cooperation with the Finance Chairman).

Finance Chairman

The finance chairman is a *fund-raiser,* in charge of raising the money needed for the campaign. He should *not* be the money dispenser, check signer or comptroller.

One of the first requirements of a good finance chairman is that he be a contributor to the campaign. It is hard to sell others on giving when you have not already given yourself.

The finance chairman should be a person of stature within the community. He should be able to meet civic leaders and other personages of importance on their own grounds. He should be able to invite leaders of the world of commerce and the professions to fund-raising affairs and have them accept on the basis of their friendship and respect for him, as well as their interest in the candidate or the cause espoused. He should also have some knowledge of *broad-base (small-gift) fund-raising* or know where to get help and advice on this part of the job of raising money.

Remember this: it is risky to select a finance chairman on the basis of name alone. Raising funds involves more than a name on a letterhead or a signature at the close of a letter. Fund-raising involves planning, the ability to prod and motivate, and a knack of organization to get others involved in helping to raise the necessary funds.

Too many campaigns make the mistake of saddling the finance chairman with the duties of treasurer. *Do not do that!* The finance chairman should not be the campaign's bookkeeper. Appoint others to those duties; let the finance chairman spend his time *raising funds.*

The finance chairman and the treasurer should have a good knowledge of the state (and/or federal) *laws governing campaign finances*—fund-raising and expenditures. If there is any question on these critical legal matters, the campaign legal counsel should be contacted immediately. Although the general campaign chairman should have a working knowledge of those laws, he must depend on the finance chairman, the treasurer and the legal counsel to *make sure the campaign does not violate either the letter or the spirit of the law.*

Treasurer

If at all possible, the campaign treasurer should be a certified public accountant. At the very least, it should be someone who has had a solid background in handling and accounting for the receipts and expenditures of funds.

The duties of the treasurer include:

—keeping the *campaign books*

—acknowledging all *campaign contributions*

—filing the official *financial statements* required by law

—assisting in the drafting of the *campaign budget* and the establishment of *cost controls* to make sure the campaign stays within that budget, and

—(if there is a paid staff) handling the *payroll* as well as paying the various *campaign bills.*

All campaign receipts and expenditures—*repeat, all*—should be channeled through the treasurer. Only in that way can the treasurer keep an up-to-date balance sheet of campaign funds and expenses, be positive that all contributions are acknowledged and reported, and be sure that all campaign expenditures are posted and reported.

It is just plain courtesy (and good public relations) to make sure that *each and every campaign contribution* is acknowledged. In the smaller campaign this can be done by a personal phone call or a personalized letter. In the larger campaign, involving thousands of small donors, a printed form is sufficient. In many campaigns, contributions over a certain amount—say $50 or $100—are recognized by a personal call or letter from the candidate.

Because of the workload involved in these details, the treasurer should probably appoint an assistant or employ a part-time secretary. In some cases the treasurer will be able to take care of these details by assigning someone from his own personal staff or office to handle certain chores.

Early in the campaign—before the campaign actually gets started, if possible—the treasurer should meet with the campaign chairman and the chairmen of the various subcommittees to *make out a budget.* At that time both the total amounts needed and the dates by which all or part of those funds are required should be determined. That will make it possible to design an *income flow chart* for use by the finance chairman and his fund-raisers.

Out of the planning sessions with the various subcommittee chairmen will come the total campaign budget, listed by activity, amount, and date required. That budget is *the basic fiscal document* for the campaign. It can be revised to meet shifting situations but it should not be bent out of shape. And, it should be regarded as both a financial guide and a planning tool

—to make sure that sufficient funds are available when needed, and

—to assure that the campaign stays within the budget and does not end up in debt.

The candidate who runs on a platform of fiscal responsibility can hardly be excused for a campaign that employs deficit spending. And, never—*never*—expect to raise money to pay off a deficit after election day has come and gone.

Some suggestions for a campaign budget are included in the section. *"All About M-o-n-e-y! Budgets and Fund-raising"* in The Appendix.

Campaign Legal Counsel

This is the committee's legal eagle. He, or she, must be a *practicing attorney* and should be familiar with those sections of the election codes and other statutes dealing with *political campaign contributions, expenditures, reports and filing dates.*

The counsel should read and give legal clearance to all speech texts, campaign literature and other important material before it is made public. *This is done to make sure that the material does not contain anything that is legally defamatory or libelous.* The legal counsel should also be alert and prepared to defend or press "political" lawsuits.

Finally, the counsel should be in charge of recruiting and deploying a corps of volunteer attorneys (and/or law students) to *assist poll watchers on election day.* After your committee has worked so hard to win the election you want to make sure it is not "stolen" at the polls.

Headquarters Chairman

Experience recommends that the headquarters chairman be a woman. This is because the person in charge of the headquarters operation is an *office manager, a secretary and a hostess-receptionist*

. . . sometimes all these things at once, sometimes one at a time. She should have had some *office experience* (so that she can evaluate workload in terms of hours required to complete a certain project), be a *good typist* (she takes care of the candidate's and campaign chairman's correspondence), be *pleasant and tactful*, and be able to *keep cool* even during the frenzy of campaign activities at the headquarters.

All work projects done in the headquarters will come under her general direction (preparing and putting out mailings, assembling precinct kits, setting up for precinct leader meetings, strategy committee sessions, etc.). And all of this on top of being a cheerful *receptionist* and pleasant voice on the *telephone*.

The headquarters should be *open every weekday* during the formal campaign, should be open *during working hours* and—especially toward the end of the campaign period—*often open at night*.

Actually, if the campaign can afford it, the best way to handle all these chores is to employ a *full-time headquarters secretary* to work under the direction of the campaign chairman or a headquarters chairman. If this is feasible, perhaps you can find someone from the church or some Christian group who can handle the job and is looking for temporary employment. If you must go outside to find a competent headquarters secretary, be sure to *check all references carefully*. The secretary must be *completely loyal* and of like-mind with the candidate and the volunteers in the campaign.

Additional details on the operation of the headquarters are covered in The Appendix (see *"The Care and Keeping of A Headquarters"*).

Materials Chairman

In the military this person would be called the *supply sergeant*. It is a job for someone who has been through a campaign before, who is good at handling details, and who can keep a running inventory of basic campaign materials and supplies.

The materials chairman has the responsibility of being sure that there are always *on hand* sufficient supplies to keep the headquarters operating smoothly and to provide materials needed by the field (precinct) forces. Those materials and supplies generally fall into three basic categories:

1. *office equipment, furnishings and machines* (desks, chairs, work tables, typewriters, postage scales, wrapping and mailing equipment, folding chairs, wastepaper baskets, etc.)

2. *basic office supplies* (paper, pencils, typewriter ribbons, pads, paper clips, mimeograph paper and ink and stencils, rubber bands, etc.)

3. *special campaign materials* (campaign literature, bumper stickers, buttons and gadgets, lawn cards, posters, mailing envelopes, postcards and even hat bands)

All of these supplies must be on hand in sufficient quantities to service precinct workers as well as headquarters personnel. There must be *one central supply center* to guarantee availability and to curb waste.

A list of basic supplies and equipment and other materials needed in a well-run headquarters is included in the section on "Headquarters".

Precinct Chairman

The precinct chairman is sales manager, field marshall and hand-holder to the troops—all-in-one.

The duties of the precinct chairman are basically six-fold:

1. *to recruit and train precinct leaders (see Chapters Nine and Ten)*

2. *to make sure that the precincts are properly organized and well-manned*

3. *to make sure the precinct captains and their blockworkers stay on target and on time* in completing their most important work (registration, voter canvassing, literature drops and get-out-the-vote drive)

4. *to make sure that enough campaign materials, and other supplies, are ordered and on hand for the precinct organization and its workers*

5. *to be the chief communications link between the campaign strategy committee and the precinct workers* (via the precinct organi-

zation chain of command). This must be a two-way communication: from the committee to the precinct workers and from the precinct workers to the committee (feedback on the public's impression of the candidate, good and bad reaction to his public position on issues, whether or not his publicity is getting to the voters, what the opponent is doing and how it is being received by the public, etc.)

6. *to assist the research chairman (and statistical analysis crew) in compiling the district's vote profile* (which will help determine where precinct workers should be deployed on a priority basis).

It is almost essential that the precinct chairman be a person who "really knows all the ropes"—has walked precincts, handled a precinct or area, etc. This not only gives the chairman a practical knowledge of the problems and needs of the precinct worker but it establishes acceptability and authority because the chairman knows "what it's all about".

Three entire chapters in this book are devoted to the job that must be done in the precincts and the way the precinct chain of command operates. Study them, know them, master them; they deal with the foundation of a winning campaign.

Public Relations Chairman

The public relations chairman is in charge of publicity, press relations and advertising. He, or she, works closely and almost constantly with the candidate and the campaign chairman (and campaign manager).

The duties of the public relations chairman fall into these areas:

1. *prepare and oversee the production of all campaign materials* (folders, flyers, brochures, bumper strips, lawn cards and posters, etc.)

2. *help draft the candidate's speeches, statements and position papers on the issues*

3. *originate, draft, produce and distribute all press statements and news releases (after they have been approved by the candidate and/or the campaign chairman and cleared by the legal counsel)*—obviously there is no need for such legal clearance of press releases on

committee appointments, opening of neighborhood headquarters, naming of town chairmen, etc., but the major releases (on issues, on comments regarding late-breaking news items, etc.) must be cleared for everyone's protection and information

4. *schedule, arrange for and conduct all press conferences* (for both the candidate and, occasionally, the campaign chairman)

5. *work to build a good professional relationship with the press*

6. *assist in the design, content, preparation, production and placement of all advertising materials* (including all media—newspapers, radio, TV, billboards, etc.)

7. *prepare the candidate's biography, background sheet and fact file, arrange for official campaign photographs and maintain a file of the selected photos, produce a press kit and any other special feature materials required to service the press or produce special campaign newspapers or newsletters*

8. *draft and prepare "one-pagers" on the candidate and campaign information for use with the precinct workers and other campaign personnel*

9. *assist the various subcommittee chairmen in preparing communication materials for their personnel or public contacts*

10. *help the campaign chairman and candidate correctly interpret and assess the findings of the public opinion polls and translate these into the required press releases, speeches, statements, etc.*

Because of the nature and importance of these responsibilities, the public relations chairman must be someone who has had experience in journalism, public relations or advertising. If at all possible the campaign should employ a *full-time public relations director* or give this exacting assignment to the agency that is handling the campaign.

Research Chairman

The basic duties of the research chairman are set forth in Chapter Eight *("The Extra-Early Start")* and are further touched upon in the special section in The Appendix *("The A-B-Cs of Statistical Analysis")*.

The research person might well be a retired individual who is an avid reader, who is up-to-date on current events (has a feel for the movement of issues) and who is eager to help in the campaign but is house-bound or cannot spend a great deal of time at headquarters.

Because of the detail work involved in the *statistical analysis* of the district, the research chairman will probably want an assistant who can help on that project. If so, accountants and women generally do the best work in compiling the data needed for the analysis. Some time will be required at the *county clerk's office* digging through past election returns and records.

The collection of the election data required for the analysis should be completed *six months before election day*. That provides enough time to prepare and analyze precinct profiles. The *precinct chairman* should arrange for volunteer help in this project (it will give those who assist a clearer picture of voter trends and habits in the various precincts).

Scheduling Chairman

The duties of this chairman have already been outlined in Chapter Seven *("The Extra-Early Start")*.

Campaigns that organize on a smaller scale and have a smaller volunteer force may want to combine scheduling and "coffees" and special events *under one chairman*. The important thing to keep in mind is that there must be one *central (master) schedule* (calendar) kept so that there are no conflicts in the candidate's appointments—and, so that you can be sure there are no long "empty" time periods and that all the important areas of the district have been covered by candidate appearances.

Special Events Chairman

Every campaign can stand some razz-ma-tazz—some colorful rallies, horn-blowing parades and other special events. They help grab public attention, they get some extra publicity for the candidate, and they give the workers a feeling that "things are really moving". Campaign volunteers like to feel they are part of a "going group"; the excitement makes them go all-out.

The special events chairman should be someone who is a bit of *a showman*—someone with a penchant for detail and drama, someone who can get people to work together; someone who may not like the tedium of office work or the public contact of precinct work but who likes to be in the center of things. There's usually at least one in every group and their capabilities can be productively used as special events chairman.

Here are a few typical special events for a campaign:

—*a kick-off rally* (or dinner) when the candidate announces the start of the formal campaign

—*picnic, barbeques or spaghetti feeds for both the precinct workers and the public*—usually held at a local park or meeting hall and designed to provide a platform for the candidate

—*parades and motorcades* (usually held on Saturday afternoons) in various towns and areas in the district

—*precinct worker rallies* (usually held early in the campaign—to get the momentum going—and again several weeks before election day—to build up a head of steam for the last big push)

—*fund-raising dinners—two types:* the first to help raise as much money as possible for the campaign treasury. *This may be a $25, $50, or even $100 a plate affair* with a prominent guest speaker, special entertainment, etc. This can be an important source of revenue and is traditional in most campaigns. But, these high-priced affairs can give the impression that the candidate is more of the "country club set" than of the people; thus, the second type of fund-raiser is important.

A pot-luck or bucket-of-fried-chicken or even box lunch affair for, at the most, five bucks a person or seven-fifty for a couple and maybe ten bucks for a family. This gives the average folks, on a tight family budget, a chance to get in on the act. Such an event should be colorful, include good family entertainment, and can often develop into a "good old fashioned revival" type get-together—song-fests, volunteer skits, etc. This type of dinner, or *a series* of them, *can be held anywhere in the district;* at the grange hall, the school cafetorium, the church basement, the veterans hall or the community center. If your candidate is truly a man of and for the people—give the people an opportunity to participate.

Remember: young people (especially teen-agers) can be a source of help on special events. They like the color and the excitement, the feeling of being in on the campaign. You can draw them into the campaign through the special events and then get them involved in putting up posters, holding mailing parties, making literature drops in supermarket parking lots, and a whole range of fun-projects.

Political action should be *a family affair,* right? Well, get the kids involved!

A final word: special events can be helpful in a campaign. *But, don't overdo them.* The extra effort in ticket sales, lining up cars and drivers for parades, decorating meeting halls, calling on the phone to promote attendance at a rally—these can help draw attention and interest to the campaign, and recruit workers for other projects, but they can also pull your workers away from other campaign jobs *that must be done.* A big rally, or too many meetings that pull the workers out of the precincts, can be self-defeating. Seek *a proper balance* between showmanship and really productive chores.

Victory Squad Chairman

Victory squads are the *auxiliary forces* that can be used to beef up the precinct organization in areas that are not fully manned. Victory squads are *special troops* pulled in for special projects such as *voter canvassing, registration drives, and get-out-the-vote campaigns on election day.* Victory squads are generally composed of individuals who want to help but do not have, or want to spend, the time involved in being a full-time precinct worker or taking a regular turn at the headquarters.

The victory squad chairman should be someone who knows where those extra-volunteers can be located, recruited, given a crash training course and put to work on *certain days in certain projects.* Usually, the victory squad chairman is a man or woman who has wide contacts with industry (management and labor) and can recruit volunteers from those sources. Other sources for victory squad manpower include the local churches, colleges, civic and service club membership rosters, youth groups, etc.

Many local chambers of commerce, trade and professional groups, and some citizens organizations (taxpayers associations and homeowner groups) have been conducting courses in public affairs and political action during recent years. The list of individuals who took those courses is another good source of volunteers for the victory squad effort.

It is essential that the victory squad chairman *coordinate* his work with the *precinct chairman.* From that liaison comes the information needed to recruit the necessary *number* of victory squad workers, and to use them *when* and *where* they are required.

Special Committees

One of the devices often used to gain additional publicity and support for the candidate is the formation of special (auxiliary) committees that endorse and recommend his election.

A list of such special committees might include:

Barbers for Smith	*Engineers* for Smith
Businessmen for Smith	*Farmers* for Smith
Businesswomen for Smith	*Lawyers* for Smith
Conservationists for Smith	*Outdoorsmen* for Smith
Doctors for Smith	*Pilots* for Smith
Educators for Smith	*Truck drivers* for Smith

Other special committees might be: *clergymen, accountants, nurses, dentists, veterans, senior citizens, youth, mobile homeowners, etc.*

Just reading the names of those suggested special committees gives you the impression that "everyone is for Smith"—*and, that's the general idea!*

Usually, these are *letterhead* committees. Sometimes members of the special committees actually get out and actively campaign. But, basically, the benefit of a special committee operation is threefold:

first, to provide additional opportunities for *publicity second,* to gain additional *attention and support* for the candidate among the various professional, trade and vocational groups in the district, and

third, to generate one more source of *campaign contributions.*

When such committees are formed, and a chairman and co-chairman and sponsoring board is recruited, a *special letterhead and envelope is printed.* (That stationery is generally paid for by the special committee members.) A letter is sent to every lawyer (or doctor, farmer, clergyman, etc., within the profession or group in the district) announcing the committee's support of the candidate and urging all members of the profession to do the same.

The mailing includes *a return envelope, an endorsement card, and a pledge card for financial contributions.*

At the same time this mailing is made, the campaign publicity (or public relations) chairman should *issue a news release* announcing the formation of the special committee, including a list of the names (and any pertinent background) on the members of the group.

If your campaign plans to have this type of special committees effort, you should appoint an individual as *special committees chairman.* The duties of that job include promoting the creation of such committees, contacting community (or district) leaders in the various professions and trades, assisting them in recruiting other members, writing the direct-mail letter and helping with the endorsement and pledge cards.

Outlying Communities Chairman

If yours is a district that spreads over a large area, and has several important outlying communities or counties that are separate and distant from the major city in which your campaign headquarters is located, you may want to open several outlying (city or county) headquarters.

If so, you should appoint an *outlying areas chairman* to coordinate that operation.

This chairman should work closely with the general campaign chairman and the precinct chairman and should be a member of the campaign strategy committee. His, or her, job is to recruit town (or county) chairmen and co-chairmen, and to assist in the location and acquisition of those outlying area headquarters.

The outlying communities chairman also acts as a liaison and chief contact between the community (or county) chairmen and the *materials chairman.* It is his, or her, responsibility to see that those headquarters have the necessary campaign literature and supplies and are kept fully advised as to the campaign schedule and any special events.

Make It A Team!

A reminder: the best campaign organization in the world is ineffective unless it is *coordinated and molded into a winning team.* So, work to engender a *positive group spirit;* make full use of the *brain power* on your strategy committee; be sure there is an effective *two-way communications* from the top to the bottom *and from the bottom to the top;* go out of your way to be sure that *each and every individual* on the team knows his, or her, work is important—*because it is!*

CHAPTER NINE

The Precinct Organization

"The whole state must be so well organized that every Whig
can be brought to the polls. So divide your county into small
districts and appoint in each a committee. Make a perfect
list of the voters and ascertain with certainty for whom they
will vote . . . Keep a constant watch on the doubtful voters
and have them talked to by those in whom they have the most
confidence. . . On election day see that every Whig is brought
to the polls."

Abraham Lincoln

In previous chapters we have touched upon the importance of
the precinct. We stressed that it is the base upon which successful
election campaigns are built; the key to political victory.

There once was an adage in American politics that "as Maine
goes, so goes the nation". That axiom no longer holds, but this
one does:

"As the precincts go, so goes the election."

Four Level Pyramid

The basic precinct organization can be described as a pyramid
with four interfacing operational layers:

1. *the district* (and the district, or campaign, precinct chairman)
2. *the region* (and the regional precinct chairman)
3. *the area* (and the area coordinator), and
4. *the precinct* (and the precinct captain and blockworkers)

The district precinct organization and the duties of the campaign precinct chairman have been outlined in *Chapter Eight* and touched on in *Chapter Seven*.

BASIC PRECINCT ORGANIZATION

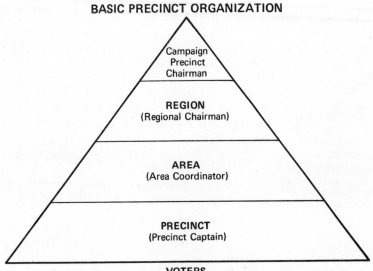

Campaign
Precinct
Chairman

REGION
(Regional Chairman)

AREA
(Area Coordinator)

PRECINCT
(Precinct Captain)

VOTERS

This four-level precinct organization structure can be modified to fit the size of the election district and the number of registered voters. It can be condensed into a two- or three-level pyramid (see section on "Tailor To Fit").

Tailor To Fit

The four-level precinct organization outlined in this and the following chapter is a full-scale structure designed to win elections in a congressional or state legislative district encompassing a large number of registered voters—anywhere from 350,000 to 500,000.

In smaller districts, with fewer registered voters and fewer precincts, the need for such a complete organization may not exist—and, the manpower may not be available. In such cases, you should tailor your precinct organization to fit the need and the circumstance. For example, a *three-level* structure may serve you best. Thus, you would go from district (or campaign) precinct chairman to area coordinator to precinct captain (omitting the regions).

Or, in an election district where there are even fewer voters and fewer precincts, a *two-level* structure may suffice. In that case you would go directly from the district precinct chairman to the precinct captains—eliminating both the regional and area levels. This might be the ideal situation in a school board race or a city council race in a small or medium-sized city.

In modifying your precinct structure, *remember this:*

Be sure that you do not overlook the essential duties that were assigned to the chairmen of the levels you have decided to omit. If you build a three-level organization and omit the regions, make sure those important responsibilities assigned to the regional chairmen are re-assigned either to the district precinct chairman or the area coordinators.

And, remember this: there are no good short cuts to building a precinct organization. Attention to detail will help assure victory.

Region

Generally there are five regions in an election district. The boundaries of a region are determined on the basis of these criteria:

1. *existing political subdivisions* (school districts, legislative districts, etc.)

2. *geography* (communities or contiguous areas, natural or psychological boundaries—a river, a freeway, a range of hills, or a socio-economic cluster)

3. *population and population dispersement* (a rural region may cover a large area yet have a smaller voter population than a metropolitan region with a high population density)

4. *ethnic group concentration*

5. *special and unique circumstances* (for example, towns with a

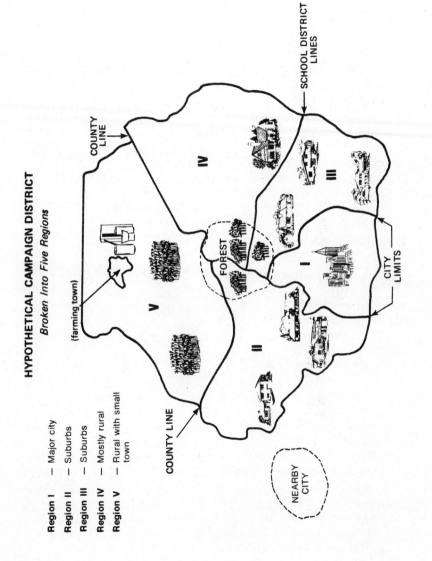

HYPOTHETICAL CAMPAIGN DISTRICT
Broken Into Five Regions

Region I — Major city
Region II — Suburbs
Region III — Suburbs
Region IV — Mostly rural
Region V — Rural with small town

strong rivalry in sports, industry or civic projects should not be lumped into the same region).

We have created a hypothetical district in which to design a typical precinct organization (see the map, "Hypothetical Campaign District", page 93). This sample district is divided into five regions and thus would have five regional precinct chairmen, one for each region.

In this hypothetical district, Region One is a *metropolitan area* that includes the central core of the largest city in the district; it has the largest voter population but, geographically, it is the smallest region. Regions Two and Three are *suburban areas.* Region Four is *mostly rural,* with a fair-sized town within its boundaries, and Region Five is *almost all rural* but includes one suburban area.

Regional Chairman

The regional chairman should be knowledgeable about the facts of political life in his jurisdiction:

—*geographical and ethnic and socio-economic groupings* within the regional boundaries

—the *important political issues* in the region and who is on which side of the issue(s)

—the *economic climate*—including employment and unemployment, job opportunities and the need for new jobs, etc.

—the *key social, service, civic and church groups* within the region (and *the leaders* of each group)

—the important *opinion leaders and molders* in the region, and

—the various *political alignments* and the size and location of the *independent and undecided voter blocs.*

The regional chairman, in other words, should have a knowledge of any situation, and group, within his area that could affect the outcome of the election. He, or she, should also know how to cope with the situation, how to get along with the various groups (or know where to go to get sound advice in this regard) and thus how to build support for the candidate.

The regional chairman must be able to drive a car, have the

ability to meet people easily and make friends, must be articulate and should be able to attend meetings on weekends and in the evenings.

Tact, diplomacy, courteous persistence, and a pleasant but firm determination to get the job done—these are essential attributes in the person who will direct the volunteer precinct organization.

And, remember this:

You cannot expect others to work hard, to make the extra effort, to put in that extra hour, unless you are willing to do so yourself.

Ideally, the regional chairman will have had previous experience in precinct work. But, an individual who has been in a position of leadership, and who has been active in community affairs, can rapidly acquaint himself, or herself, with the goals, techniques and tools of precinct work and the concept of political organization.

Recruiting Regional Chairmen

Where do you find those five key individuals to be regional precinct chairmen? Here are some possibilities:

—*political associates* from earlier campaigns

—*friends at the church* (congregation, Bible class, etc.)

—*community leaders* (who have been active in Salvation Army Red Cross, March of Dimes, etc.)

—*business or professional acquaintances* (who have been active in community affairs or who are now willing to become active)

—*middle-aged or older couples* (whose children are now grown and thus can take a more active role in public affairs) and

—*young marrieds* (who have not yet started a family but want to help build a better community, a better state or nation, for the children they plan to have).

You can find just the right individuals. Put your mind to work. *Pray about it.* You will find that you know many more capable persons than you realized.

And many of them, if not most, are just as disenchanted and just as upset as you are about the way things have been going. Sell them on the idea of getting active in good government. Remind them of Congressman John Conlan's admonition: *"Participate,*

Christian! Participate!"

Or, recall for them the Scripture's account of Abraham and his plea to the Lord to spare Sodom, and the Lord's final offer:

"I will not destroy it, for ten's sake." That's what the Lord said: ten good people and He would save the city.

If they are leary of any good coming of political work, if they are pessimistic, convinced that "things are too far gone" and there is no hope, remind them of how the Lord opened the way for Joshua and his people at the battle of Jericho. How those walls came tumbling down because they heard God's call, and followed his instructions—*and had faith.*

Or, what about Gideon and his 300? How they routed the 135,000! Remember God's promise? *"Five of you shall chase a hundred, and a hundred of you shall put ten thousand to flight . . .".*

Five good regional chairmen working in concert with a dynamic campaign organization and backed by dedicated precinct captains and workers *can elect* righteous men and women to public office.

Duties Of The Regional Chairman

The regional chairman recruits, trains and supervises the division chairmen in his region.

He, or she, is the liaison, the chief link, between the campaign precinct chairman and the division leaders. He keeps the division chairmen up-to-date on campaign strategy and schedules, makes sure they receive the campaign materials they need, and is the trouble shooter for the region. On request of a precinct captain he speaks at precinct meetings, and answers the sticky questions and gives advice on how to overcome the more difficult problems in the precincts.

He, or she, coordinates the precinct activities in the region with the campaign calendar of events. This includes the pre-planned schedule for voter canvassing, registration drives, literature drops, and inventorying voter needs (baby sitters and transportation on election day, absentee ballots, etc.) as well as the final get-out-the-vote drive, the deployment of victory squads and the election day work.

Tools For The Regional Chairman

In larger campaigns, the regional chairman should be provided with an office. This is generally located in the candidate's headquarters in one of the outlying communities within the region. If such an office is not available, the regional chairman should be willing to make his, or her, home the central command post for the precinct work in the region.

The working tools for the region chairman include:

—a copy of the *state election codes* and the *state manual* that is published as a supplement to this text

—a *map of the region* showing the precinct boundaries

—a master set of *voter registration lists* (index sheets) for the region

—a *phone and address book* with the names, phone numbers and addresses of all workers in the region

—*campaign stationery*

—*campaign literature and materials,* and

—an *organizational chart* showing the names of all campaign workers in the region, plus an organizational chart showing the names and positions of all key campaign chairmen, and their home and office phone numbers.

The Area

Each of the five regions in our typical district precinct structure is organized into areas. The number of precincts included within an area varies and is determined by the various factors and circumstances within the region. The rule of thumb is:

design your structure so that it is realistic, and practical.

If a region comprises 100 precincts, it could be divided into ten areas of ten precincts each. *Territory* is, again, a matter of prime consideration. Your district might have fewer, and larger, areas if it is rural; it might have more, and smaller areas if it is urban.

Manpower is also a key factor. It might be ideal to have ten areas with ten precincts each. But, what if you cannot find ten individuals qualified and willing to serve as area coordinators? Then you will have to settle on—say—eight areas with from 12 to 13 precincts, each, or perhaps even five areas composed of 20 precincts, each. It is far better to have fewer areas, and fewer area coordinators, than to have a pretty organization chart with lots of areas but a number of weak coordinators—or no coordinator at all in several of the areas.

The Area Coordinator

In recruiting your area coordinator, review the potential sources and qualifications listed for regional chairmen. Some individuals on that list who might not be willing, or quite ready, to accept a regional responsibility might be willing to serve at the area level.

One other, and important source: at the area level *husband-and-wife teams* can be most effective. Also, they can operate effectively and conveniently out of their own homes.

Married couples, especially those with children, are usually deeply concerned about the state of the nation, the state or community. They tend to be aware of government affairs and civic events as they affect their income and purchasing power, their home, the safety of their children and themselves, and the quality of education.

The wife may have time during the day, while the kids are at school, to attend the various precinct meetings. She and her husband can then work as a team during the evenings and on weekends. This is a matter of organization and any woman who runs a home is, by the very nature of that task, a good organizer.

Duties Of The Area Coordinator

The area coordinator
  —*recruits, trains and supervises* the precinct captains
  —*coordinates campaign projects, drives and special events* within the area
  —*transmits information, materials and supplies, and the details*

of the campaign schedule from the regional chairman to the precinct captains, and

—*keeps constant watch over the precincts* to make sure the work is being done effectively—and on time.

The area coordinator holds regular meetings, and *workshops,* for the precinct captains and their blockworkers, reviews the most effective *techniques for covering precincts,* advises them on recruitment and training of additional precinct workers, and serves as the precinct representative in meetings with the regional and district precinct leaders.

The area coordinator (or, in the case of a husband-and-wife team, one of the team) will be expected to attend district-wide precinct meetings. In a well-run campaign these meetings are held to a minimum so that the precinct personnel can spend their time organizing and working their precincts.

Tools

It is essential that the area coordinator have, and keep up-to-date, the following tools and materials:

—a *map of the area* (and colored pins) to indicate those precincts that are manned by captains and blockworkers

—a *phone book with the names, addresses and phone numbers* of all precinct workers in the area (and the names and phone numbers of the regional precinct chairman and the campaign headquarters staff)

—*extra campaign supplies* (as a source of supply for precinct captains)

—a *card index file and chart* of the precinct captains, precinct blockworkers and notations of progress (work done/not done, etc.), and

—*basic supplies* (pencils, cards, rubber bands, voter canvassing sheets, etc.). These can be obtained from the regional chairman and should always be on hand in sufficient quantities to service the precinct workers at a moment's notice.

On To The Precinct!

We have now worked our way to the base—the foundation—of the precinct structure: *the precinct,* and the work that must be done by the precinct captains and the blockworkers.

This work is so vital, and the materials involved of such importance, that they deserve—and are given—a chapter of their own.

After all, the organization and detail and materials we have built so far were all designed with one purpose in mind:

recruiting, directing and servicing the precinct workers.

CHAPTER TEN

The Winning Place

"All politics stems from the precinct. If you can't win a precinct, you can't win a nation."

Jake Arvey *

To review: the precinct is the smallest and the mightiest unit in the political structure. It is established by law. Its size and boundaries and its number of potential voters are established by the county election officials to facilitate voter convenience and to expedite the collection and tally of the votes cast.

Usually precincts are drawn to include an average of from 500 to 700 registered voters. They may be smaller—and they may go as high as 1,000 registered voters in high-density population areas.

The Typical Precinct Structure

For ease and effectiveness in operations, you should divide your precinct into *blocks* formed by roads and streets and their intersec-

---

* Jacob M. Arvey, one-time Democratic National Committeeman from Illinois. For many years he was considered the political boss in Cook County (Chicago).

tions. When a block is heavily populated, the ideal is to recruit one precinct worker per block (called a *blockworker*). If the area is not so heavily populated, two or three or four blocks may be combined into a unit and assigned to a blockworker or a team of blockworkers (or, a husband-and-wife team).

In a metropolitan area, where the population is especially concentrated and one or two blocks could constitute a precinct, the political organization may call for one or two blockworkers in each high-rise apartment building. However, the basic precinct structure and chain of command remains pretty much the same.

The organizational chart for a typical precinct might look something like this:

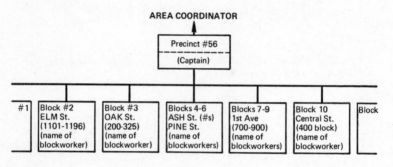

The Precinct Captain

The precinct captain is the key member of the precinct team. It is his, or her, job to organize, and operate, the precinct work so that the maximum number of votes are delivered for the candidate on election day. Hopefully, this will be a majority of the votes cast. Sometimes, because of party registration and longstanding voter habits, this will not be possible. But, even in a precinct oriented toward the opposition, *every vote counts*. Getting the maximum number of votes for your candidate may not win the precinct but it *can make the difference* in carrying the county, or the district . . . or, the state!

Qualifications Of The Precinct Captain

The precinct captain must be a person with a strong sense of purpose; an individual who radiates enthusiasm for his, or her, cause—enough enthusiasm to keep going day-after-day, even when the going gets rough. *And, the precinct person should be an organizer, a self-starter and one who sticks with a job until it is done.*

There are many individuals in every neighborhood who would make great precinct captains. Folks who are warm, friendly, concerned and conscientious. But, they may be reluctant to get into politics at the precinct level.

Well, before you take "No" for their answer, encourage them to reconsider. Point out the opportunity for service, the opportunity to expand themselves, to develop new skills. And, remind them: *they will not be alone!*

You might share with them this story from the life of Arthur Langlie, a former governor of the state of Washington.

Years ago, Gov. Langlie, who was active in the Christian Business Men's Committee, was touring his state and found himself in a small town with an hour to spare. For some time he had been hearing about a member of CBMC who lived in that town, a man who was a real dynamo in Christian work. Langlie had wanted to meet that man and here was his opportunity!

The governor drove to the man's home and introduced himself to the man's wife. He apologized for calling without an appointment but wondered if it would be possible to meet her husband and share a few moments with him. As Art Langlie sat in the living room, waiting, he thought about all the things this man had done for Christ and he tried to envision what the man would look like: a vital, dynamic individual; a person of strong bearing and impressive stature; a man among men.

The gentleman who entered the living room did not fit Gov. Langlie's mental picture—not in the slightest. He was short, frail, stooped; his face was etched and pinched with the lines of a long and painful illness; his eyes were obscured by the thick lenses of his glasses. He walked with the aid of a cane and each step was a torturous victory of spirit over body.

Gov. Langlie rose with a start and the man read his thoughts.

His smile broadened into a chuckle. He balanced himself on his cane and stuck out his hand:

"Governor! *Isn't it wonderful what the Lord can use?*"

Duties

The precinct captain must use all of his, or her, enthusiasm to recruit others and to imbue them with a sense of purpose and a will to persist. In recruiting blockworkers, the captain must be sure to:

—acquaint them with the *personal and political philosophy* of the candidate

—*recruit them* on the basis of their enthusiasm in support of that philosophy and the candidate, and

—explain to them in detail the *duties and techniques* of a block-worker (or, get them a copy of this book):

1. the how-to of *voter canvassing*
2. the *precinct tools* available and how those tools can be used in door-to-door work
3. the how-to of *gathering important voter information* from every adult resident in every home in their assigned block(s)
4. *the campaign schedule*
5. the proven *techniques of precinct "saleswork";* how to "sell" the candidate's qualities, programs and policies and how to "sell" the voter on supporting the candidate
6. the various *election-day duties* and *get-out-the-vote details,* and
7. the need for an *on-going precinct and block organization* after the election and during off-election periods

The conscientious precinct captain will keep the precinct card files up-to-date as voter information is gleaned by the blockworkers. Based on that information, and a general knowledge of the precinct, the captain will inform the area coordinator of any election-day *victory squad* assistance needed to:

—help *get out the vote*

—serve as *pollwatchers,* and

—help *provide voter services* (baby sitters, transportation to and from the polls, etc.).

Other precinct captain duties include:

—attending *area precinct meetings* (to keep abreast of developments)

—holding *blockworker meetings* to relay campaign information and to attend to the necessary record-keeping chores, and

—organizing the troops for *special projects* and voter canvasses.

And, in addition to all of that, the wise precinct captain will find time to occasionally get out and *walk part of the precinct*—go door-to-door with the blockworkers. Setting the example is an important part of exercising leadership; it is also a vital element of Christian life.

Deputy Registrars

An efficient precinct captain will recruit someone in the precinct to qualify and serve as a *deputy registrar of voters.* This is important. It provides an added convenience for the unregistered voters located by the blockworkers and it provides greater assurance that those friendly unregistered citizens will register and will vote on election day.

Election Boards

The precinct captain should also keep tabs on the appointment of individuals to the *precinct election board.* It is important to ascertain whether that board is "balanced"—whether the political parties have equal representation on the board. If there is an imbalance, if the precinct captain's party is not properly represented on that election board, the county clerk should be notified of that fact. And, the precinct captain should help to recruit an applicant to serve on the board so that it is in proper balance. Election board workers are usually paid a small fee for their day's work.

Recruiting Blockworkers

Where do you get your blockworkers? How do you find them—and enough of them to cover every block in your precinct?

Start with friends, with neighbors, with the folks down the street who go to church or belong to a Bible study group. Will they serve as blockworkers? You'll never know until you ask them!

And, since we are working to build one nation under God, why not start with God's basic social unit—*the family?* Get the families involved.

Far too many political campaigns have left—and still leave—ruptured families in their wake; husbands and wives estranged, widened gaps between parents and children. Some well-intentioned folks have been so busy saving the world they have lost their families. We cannot build a strong and stable nation if we weaken or destroy family ties; our work is to build the family unit, not wreck it!

Try to *recruit married couples* to join as one, to work as a team. That not only expands the precinct work, it helps to strengthen the family.

Older children (teen-agers) should be encouraged to work with their parents to help on special events, help stuff envelopes or prepare voter information packets, deliver supplies, help put up posters and lawn cards—or serve as baby sitters on election day (and even during precinct meetings). All of this work adds up to an excellent (and satisfying) education in good government and the responsibilities of citizenship.

TOOLS FOR THE BLOCKWORKER

The proper tools are essential if the blockworkers are to do the most effective job. It is an important part of the precinct captain's responsibilities to make sure that those tools are available—in sufficient quantities and at the proper times.

The balance of this chapter deals with those tools, what they are, and how to use them.

Voter Index Lists

These are the large, official sheets of paper on which are printed in alphabetical order the name and address of every registered voter in the precinct. The sheets are prepared and produced by the county clerk or the registrar of voters—usually from computer tapes in the county offices. You may have noticed these sheets—the ones for your precinct—tacked on the wall outside your polling place on election day.

The index sheet you will probably be using in your pre-primary work—especially if you start early in your efforts—will be a carry-over from the previous general election. That means it will be at least a year old and therefore it will not reflect all the changes that have occured since then; families that have moved away, new families that have moved in, deaths, and those young people who have reached the voting age.

If you live in a fairly settled (stable) community, one in which there is not much moving around, changes in the voter list will be minimal. If, however, you live in a larger city or an area where there is a high population turn-over—where a high percentage of the families change residence periodically—you will have a bit of work to do to *keep your voter index sheet up-to-date.*

But, that detail is most important: the up-to-date index sheet is the basis from which you build your precinct card file and chart your precinct map. And, as we will mention later on, that up-to-date card file can be of real importance for poll watching on election day.

Precinct Map

A precinct map shows the boundaries of the precinct, the streets (or portions of streets) within those boundaries, and the houses (by the numbers) located within the precinct area.

If your division chairman does not provide you with such a precinct map, *make your own.* A map of the area in which your precinct lies can usually be obtained from either the county clerk or the county engineer or planning department. Be sure the map shows *both* the streets and houses, by number.

Taking the address information from the index sheets, *draw the boundaries of the precinct.* Trace the lines lightly at first until you are positive you have the lines drawn correctly. Be careful to draw those lines so that they include *exactly* the streets, portions of streets and house numbers listed within the district. Quite often a precinct boundary will run down the middle of a street so that the houses on one side are in one precinct and the houses on the opposite side are in the adjacent precinct. Pay particular attention to this.

When you have completed mapping the boundaries of your precinct, mount the map on a piece of plywood or heavy cardboard or tack it on the wall in a prominent place in your work area. You will refer to it constantly during the campaign.

Use map pins to show those blocks that are covered by workers. Use different colored pins to indicate the blockworkers who are doing a good job, those who are doing a marginal job (and need jacking up), and those who are doing a poor job. For example:

—green pin—*good* job (work done on time and done well)
—white pin—*marginal* job (a little late, but work well done)
—black pin—*poor* job (falling behind, work inaccurate or incomplete)
—red pin—*no worker* (recruit one!)

Blockworker Chart

Take a sheet of tablet or typing paper and mark it into three columns. Working left-to-right, print at the head of column one, *"Street and House Numbers";* at the top of column two, *"Blockworker's Name",* and at the top of column three, *"Blockworker's Address and Phone Number".*

Now transfer the information from your precinct map to the chart. In *column one,* list the street name(s) and house numbers— making a separate entry in the column for each block. In *column two,* opposite the block entry, list the name of the person(s) assigned to that block. In *column three,* enter the address and phone number of the blockworker(s).

Your blockworker chart will look something like this:

Street & House Numbers	Blockworker's Name	Blockworker's Address & Phone Number
First Avenue (1101-1167)	John & Mary Jones	1139 First Avenue 620-3654
Oak Street (2346-2348)	Ann Hopkins	2347 Oak Street 620-2587

List all of the blocks in the precinct in column one. Opposite to those entries, list the names and addresses and phone numbers of all your blockworkers. As you recruit additional blockworkers for blocks not yet covered, *add those new names to your chart.*

Card Files

The efficient precinct captain uses *two card files* (3″ x 5″ is the most convenient size):
—the *"house"* card file, and
—the *"name"* card file.
Taking the information from your index sheet, *make a separate card for each address* (house number, apartment number, etc.) *on every street* in your precinct.
Print (or type) the street name and house number at the top of the card. Under it, record the name of *each registered voter* listed at that address. File these cards alphabetically *by street name* and then file the cards for that street numerically, *by house number.*
This is an example of how such a *"house card"* looks:

```
ELM STREET        #936

Smith, Harry
Smith, Belle
```

Now, the second set of file cards—the *"name cards"*.

Back to the index sheet again! *Make out a file card for each and every registered voter in the precinct.* Make *a separate card* for each voter at each address.

Record (print or type) the name of the voter at the top of the card (last name first). Under the name write the address. If two or more registered voters with the same last name reside at the address—such as a husband and wife and son or daughter of voting age—you can get away with only one card *but be sure to list all three voters.* However, if persons with *different last names* reside at the same address (a relative, an in-law, a boarder), *make a separate name card for each of those individual voters.*

File these cards *alphabetically,* by name. In your spare time look up the *phone numbers* and record these on the cards. Better yet, ask someone in your family (husband, son, daughter) to help with that chore. Do this early in the campaign so that the cards are ready when you need them.

This is an example of how a *"name"* card looks:

```
┌─────────────────────────────────────────────┐
│                                               │
│   SMITH, HARRY        620-5938                │
│   SMITH, BELLE                                │
│   SMITH, EILEEN                               │
│        936 Elm Street                         │
│                                               │
│                                               │
└─────────────────────────────────────────────┘
```

Updating Card Files

Before primary election day—usually three to four weeks be-fore—the precinct captain should receive (from the area coordinator) *the latest voter index sheets.* Using the "name" card file made earlier in the campaign, *check the card file against the new index sheet.* If there are any conflicts or discrepancies, *mark these on the index sheet.*

This is important!

The county clerk cannot remove a registered voter's name from the index sheet until and unless that voter failed to cast a ballot in the previous general election. However, the precinct captain who has kept his, or her, card files up-to-date will know who has moved out of the precinct, who has died, etc., since that election. The precinct captain knows, in other words, who is and who is not eligible to vote in the precinct.

Errors in the index sheet should be made known to those volunteers who will serve as poll watchers on election day. The information will enable the poll watcher to challenge any citizen who tries to cast a ballot for a voter who has moved out of the precinct or whose mortal remains now rest in the cemetery.

Poll watching, and challenging the illegal voter, is a legal and important way to protect the sanctity of the ballot box and the franchise of every properly registered voter. Too many ballot boxes have been stuffed with votes cast by individuals whose names had long since been chiseled in headstones. *Don't let it happen in your precinct.*

If you cannot get the latest index sheet in time to check it against your card files prior to election day, go to the polls early on that morning and check your card files against the index sheet that will be posted, by law, near the door of the polling place. Courtesy should prompt you to introduce yourself to the senior clerk on the precinct election board and to explain what you are there to do. There should be no objection to checking the index sheet as long as you *do not interfere with the voting process.*

Blockworkers' Kit

The precinct captain should obtain enough heavy paper or plastic folders so that there is *one kit for each blockworker* in the precinct. These folders should have "pockets" on either or both the inside front and back covers. Your area coordinator should be able to obtain these folders for you. If the campaign cannot supply them, they can be purchased at the local five-and-dime, or supermarket.

On the *outside* of the front cover, print the blockworker's name. On the *inside* front cover, paste a sheet on which is written the name of the street and the street numbers of the houses assigned to that blockworker. Make up one of these folders, with lists, for each of the blockworkers in the precinct. The kit, and the streets and houses on the list, are the blockworker's responsibility for the remainder of the campaign.

The kit should include a pencil, any canvassing instruction sheets, and any materials needed for the canvassing work. And, it should include a detail sheet for that block (or, those blocks) "charged" to that individual blockworker.

Blockworker's Detail Sheet

At the top of a standard sheet of typing or tablet paper, print or type the street name and the numbers of the houses included in the block. Under that draw *three columns,* left to right. At the top of column one, print *"House Number".* At the top of column two, print *"Voter's Name".* At the top of column three, print *"Comments".*

The third column will be used by the blockworker to record any important notes about the voters in his block—"Registered *(party)",* "Not Registered", "Independent", "Potential Worker", "Will need baby sitter on election day", etc. The information recorded in column three is very important; *it is the key to your vote-getting work.*

This is an example of how a blockworker's detail sheet (or, "Canvassing Information Sheet") might look:

ELM STREET - 100 thru 142

House Number	Voter's Name	Comments
100	Johnson, Rich & Dot	Both regis. GOP. Mrs. J. will work election day
102	Gillespie, Dick & Pat	Neither registered, but friendly and interested
104	Brody, Jim	Regis. Dem. Votes party

The blockworkers detail sheet is placed *in the pocket of the kit,* and given to him, or her. It is then the blockworker's responsibility to keep that sheet up-to-date, adding to it and revising the information as the campaign progresses.

The sheet is turned into the precinct captain *at the completion of each precinct project* during the campaign. From the information on that sheet, the precinct captain can up-date the card files. After the data have been copied on the file cards, the sheets are returned to the blockworkers for future use.

A tip to help the precinct captain:

It would take the precinct captain hours and hours to copy the data from the blockworker detail sheets on the file cards. Why not have *a coffee klatch* for the blockworkers and let each one transfer the information on his or her detail sheet to your corresponding cards?

The same technique could be followed while preparing the blockworker's kits. *Everyone get together and pitch in; many hands, light work, etc.*

Under no circumstances should blockworkers take the master card files from the precinct captain's home. Those cards are the gold in your political bank; the logistical information vital to victory. If lost or destroyed, it would take hours and hours to remake them.

Address Book

The precinct captain should have an address book with the names and addresses and phone numbers of *all key campaign* people (at the district, region and area levels). This book should include both home and business addresses and phone numbers and should be made up for the precinct captain by the campaign headquarters.

Canvassing Technique Sheet

For each precinct activity (registration drive, voter canvass, literature drop, etc.) *a special one-pager* should be prepared setting forth the details of the project and the suggested methods to be followed.

Those sheets, one for each blockworker, should be produced by the region or area precinct leaders and distributed in sufficient quantities to the precinct captains. The precinct captains, in turn, hand these out to their blockworkers with any additional instructions.

The blockworker should keep those pages in his or her kit for ready-reference.

Calendar of Campaign Events

This is the campaign timetable or master calendar. It is prepared by the campaign headquarters and sets forth the major events that have been scheduled throughout the campaign. These calendars are produced in sufficient quantities so that *each and every member* of the precinct organization has a copy.

Reverse Telephone Directory

A reverse telephone directory can make life a lot easier for the precinct captain and the blockworkers.

These reverse directories list telephone numbers *by street name and house number* (and, give the subscriber's name). With one of those directories, it takes only a few minutes to list the phone numbers for every house on the block.

The reverse phone directory is no substitute for the blockworker's information gained through the door-to-door canvass. It should be used only when there is no worker available in certain blocks.

City Register

Many cities and towns have what is known as a *city register.* This book contains the names of all members of a family residing at each address in the city, lists the means of livelihood of the wage-earners, and their place of employment, and can often be used in determining a voter's political leanings or philosophical persuasions.

List of Deputy Registrars

A list of all available deputy registrars in the area, with their addresses and phone numbers, should be part of the blockworker's kit. The list should also include the address and phone number of those locations at which registrars and deputy registrars are on duty (county clerk's office, firehouses, libraries, etc.)

Once a blockworker has contacted an unregistered resident who wants to register, information on registrars should be readily available to help answer any questions. Get your voters registered. *Remember:* one vote could make the difference!

Availability of Materials

All of the basic materials mentioned in this chapter should be produced by the campaign headquarters and made readily and easily available to all precinct workers through the precinct chain of command.

Make sure that is the case in your campaign. Remember the old adage: for want of a nail, a shoe, a horse, a message . . . *and the battle was lost.* Don't let that happen to you. Plan ahead!

If for any reason these materials are not available from the campaign headquarters—if yours is a smaller campaign with a handful of volunteers and a make-do situation—don't be dismayed. *Use your ingenuity, make your own.* Make what you need for your particular situation, and use it well.

With the exception of the index sheets (voter registration lists) and the reverse telephone directory and city register, most of the materials can be purchased or made for pennies—or, dimes.

If necessary, ask the blockworker to purchase the folder, etc.

Perhaps someone in the group has a mimeograph or copying machine at home or in the office; borrow it to run off your canvass information sheets, etc.

Where there is a will there will be a way. Do what must be done so that together all of us can do what must be done to transform our precincts, our districts, our counties and states and our nation into a great government, of and by and for the people under God.

CHAPTER ELEVEN

Do Thou Likewise . . .

"... and if there be any other commandment, it is briefly comprehended in this saying, namely, Thou shalt love thy neighbor as thyself".

Romans 13:9

So far, in the chapters on precincts, we have examined the building of the organization and outlined the political work to be done by the captains and the kings (the blockworkers).

And, in most books on politics that would be it; the precinct is generally looked upon as simply the place where you work to get out the vote.

But to the Christian the precinct must be more than maps and index sheets and card files and election day activities. *The precinct should be a place of service.*

What's that you say, service? Man, that's different!

That's right, it is different. And, Christians are, or should be, different. Remember what we said, early in this book: Christians should get into politics *to transform, not conform.*

The Christian in politics should be just as concerned—in fact, even more concerned—about helping those in need as he is about getting out the vote. The neighbor down the street who needs help, the widow who is ill or lonely, the father who is out of a job, the teen-ager in trouble; these, too, must be our concern.

It is simply a matter of applied Christianity.

"Thou shalt love thy neighbor as thyself . . ."

Love one another. Help one another. Even the least of these. Is it too much to expect Christians to apply *I Corinthians 13:1-13* in their precinct work as in all other work? Certainly not!

For, if we do all good things to build a better nation and a better government—and have not love, compassion, concern—it will profit us little; it will be as nothing . . . a tinkling cymbal and a sounding brass.

Old-time Politics

The Bible is replete with admonitions and examples of how we are to put our love to work in everyday affairs; how we are to help and comfort our fellow men.

If those commandments and teachings are not sufficient to motivate us, consider the examples of the old-time politicians—the men and women who practiced the art of politics in America long before television and radio and campaign consultants and image-making took over.

Years ago, when a family moved into the precinct or ward, the party worker was there to greet the new arrivals; to help them get settled, to make them feel at home. It was sort of a political "welcome wagon" operation. Often the political worker would see to it that the family had hot meals until the gas was turned on, or see that they had extra bedding until their own arrived.

In those days the political machines were service organizations. Granted that was no doubt the best way to deliver the votes. Granted the end-results of those machine operations left much to be desired and many things to be rejected. The fact is, the services were rendered and the individuals were helped.

If Junior fell ill, the ward man saw to it that the doctor came and that the bill was paid or guaranteed. If the father lost his job, the ward man could usually help him find work. If the plumbing needed fixing, or the street lights went out, or the family got behind on the rent, the politician was there to do what he could; at least he tried to help.

Jake Arvey, one-time political boss of Chicago, put it this way: "What makes the political organization effective? *Service!*"

In writing about "The Successful Political Organization", Arvey described how he and the members of his machine built a strong and powerful party in Cook County. He pointed out that in many instances they could have depended on the public agencies but that they knew *the personal touch was more effective.*

Arvey and his group delivered baskets of food and bundles of clothes and medicine for the sick. They went out and raised money. They got donations from the wealthy, they held money-making benefits, and they used the proceeds to help those in need. They organized child-care centers, they kept kids out of jail, and they got their parents jobs.

Wrote Arvey: "It got so that . . . neighbors would call us and say, 'You know the people who live in the basement in my building? They're bad off. They don't have coal, they don't have any food, and there is nobody working.' And we would go in there and give them aid, without checking anything like party affiliation. We would check later, *but we gave them immediate help.*"

If Jake Arvey and his machine could do so much in the pursuit of political power, *how much more should we do in the practice of Christian love?* Faith, yes. But faith without works—and work without love? Love is the fulfilling of God's law!

Love one another . . . love thy neighbor as thyself . . . for as much as you do it unto the least of these, you do it unto Me!

Some may say the type of services provided by Jake Arvey and company are out of style now; relics of a different era. Things are different now, the needs do not exist.

How wrong they are! *Never was there a greater need!* All over this nation—in the suburbs as well as the slums—individuals are crying out for help. They need food for the body and food for the soul. Where would you have them turn? What would you have them do?

What is the proper role of the Christian in public affairs?

There are those who preach the social action gospel. They are surely well-intentioned but all too often what they really expound is government action. There are times and circumstances where government action is needed, and proper. *But, Caesar and his agencies are no substitue for Christian love.* To rely so much on Caesar is to belittle God . . . and to duck our personal responsibilities; that is what has happened in far too many areas today. We have made the state the shepherd and we reap the consequences—not only in a shriveled soul but also in excessive taxation, rampant inflation, and controlled citizens and uncontrolled government.

True social action is not more government action, *it is personal action.* Individual effort. Christian love on a one-to-one basis. Love in action.

Love in Action

In Sacramento, California, a group of Christian young people put their love to work. They used their time and talents to help an elderly widow repair and paint her tiny cottage. They bought the nails, the wood, the paint and brushes; they did the work; they gave of themselves. And, that was just the start. They went on from there to help other families in the area fix up their homes.

In another city, church members turned the empty lot next to the Sunday School building into a vegetable garden. They tilled the soil and planted the seeds and watered and weeded and gathered the harvest and brought it as a love offering to the residents of a nearby old folks home. What was not eaten fresh during the season was canned for their winter months.

In yet another town, the ladies of a Bible study group learned that a family in the neighborhood was going down and under; the father was out of work, the money was gone, the bills were piling up, there was hardly enough food for the kids, and the lending institution was about to fore-close the mortgage. The ladies went into Christian action. Baskets of food appeared on the family's doorstep. Boxes of clothes for the children arrived out of nowhere. There were gifts of money; some neighbors offered loans. And on Christmas eve a frozen turkey and all the fixings—plus gifts for the children—just managed to find its way into the kitchen while the family attended church services.

And, in other areas:

—young high school students take their time to make weekly visits to a children's hospital to read to the patients and otherwise entertain them

—a group of retired folks have become "foster grandparents" to the mentally retarded children at a state hospital

—a Christian lady and her friends beg, borrow, wheedle and scrounge food and cooking utensils, heat and light, to provide daily hot lunches for hundreds of school children in an impoverished area of their community

—Christian doctors and dentists and nurses run free clinics for the poor and the sick and work evenings and weekends at the clinic or on house calls

—sewing circles, baking parties, nursery schools and child-care centers, a volunteer job-placement service run by Christian businessmen . . .

. . . and, in Lynden, Washington, when the Concerned Christian Citizens there are not working the precincts they are operating a half-way house to help convicts released from the nearby state prison to find jobs and start new lives.

The list of such applied Christianity is long, but not long enough. Because, the list of unmet need for Christian love and help is even longer. What about the need in your precinct? Or, in your district?

Unfortunately too many Christians think they have attended to the major part of their social responsibilities through the taxes they pay—and the taxes they vote to have others pay. Somewhere along the line we have allowed Caesar to rewrite the Golden Rule: "Do unto others . . . *by proxy*". Love through a governmental agency, love by proxy, is all too often the plastic answer these days.

That kind of love through a middleman can lead to all sorts of problems—personal and public.

In one of his essays in his lovely little book, *"What Can A Man Do?"*, Milton Mayer tells the story of two men recalling one of their luncheon meetings during the great depression. As they had been enjoying that meal at an expensive restaurant, a man, gaunt with hunger and chilled by the wind, stopped outside the window by their table. In his arms he held a child, hollow-eyed, blue, and sick with hunger. The man pressed his face against the glass and looked in. He did not beg. He only stood and stared at the plates of food, the basket of bread, the cups of hot coffee. Then he was gone.

Recounting the experience years later, one of the men explained: "I couldn't give him half my steak but I could vote for Roosevelt and the WPA got them off the street."

Well, perhaps the WPA did get "them" off the street. But taxes, and taking from Paul to help Peter, is no substitute for personal love and Christian action. Conscience is not always the companion of compassion; frequently it is a cop-out.

In contrast to the men at the restaurant, consider the Good Samaritan. There was no love by proxy there, no middleman. *The Good Samaritan gave of himself.* Where others had hurried by, he stopped; he knelt in the dirt and dust of the road and ministered to the stricken stranger; he gave of his food and water and ointments. He carried the fevered man to the village and gave the inn-keeper of his own substance to pay for the stranger's care until he should be well again.

What a need there is today for more Good Samaritans—in the precincts as well as in the churches.

What has all this to do with politics and precinct work?

Well, it means that in all things—including politics—we should be about our Father's business—as the *first* order of business.

And, it means that when we start serving God by serving others we can start pushing Caesar back to where he belongs. In that way we can restore the balance in government and once again render to Caesar only that which is properly Caesar's, and unto God all that which is truly His.

Love one another . . .

For as much as you do these things unto the least of these . . .

You do it unto Me.

Go, thou, and do likewise . . . make your precinct efforts count—for *both* God and country!

CHAPTER TWELVE

The Campaign Timetable

"Expect great things from God; attempt great things for God."
William Carey
Founder,
Baptist Missionary Society
1792

Okay! We have the campaign organization—*the winning team*—under way and coming together. Let's consider the campaign timetable.

Planning ahead is all-important!

Timing is essential!

Let's start to do both, *now.*

Presented here is a full-scale and fully-detailed campaign timetable. It is designed for a winning campaign in a large congressional or state legislative district. It may well be that you and your committee will not have the time or manpower or resources to follow it in every detail. And, it may be that you will not need such an extensive calendar to win your campaign. Tailor your timetable to fit your circumstances.

Just remember: start as early as you can, do as much as you can, include as many details as you need—and, whatever your campaign timetable, stay on schedule so that you reach your goal on election day.

The Six Phases of A Campaign

There are six different phases of a campaign. All are inter-related and each builds on those that have gone before. But, each has its own *pace* and its own *projects*. So, let's outline each one.

Get yourself at least six sheets of paper. Print these headings at the top of the paper, starting with sheet one and going through sheet six:

1. *The Extra-Early Period* (10-16 months ahead)
2. *The Running Start* (6-8 months ahead)
3. *The Grand Opening* (the last 60 days)
4. *The Big Sell* (the last 30 days)
5. *The Fast Close* (the last 15 days)
6. *Election Day* (and the date)

On each of the sheets of paper list all of those basic and major projects and activities that must be done during the particular phase of the campaign. To ascertain those items, go back and check through the various chapters in this book:

Especially Chapter Seven *("The Extra-Early Start")* and the chapters on building the candidate and the winning team. Review the chapters on precinct organization and operations, itemize those chores and the dates involved. *Then add your own ideas.*

The first time around, list these projects on the correct sheet in any order—as you come across them in the chapters, as they come to mind, etc. Don't worry about whether they are put down in the correct sequence, just get them down on paper. After you have listed all the projects for each of the six campaign periods, then redo your sheets; this time try to get them in order or time sequence (the dates on which the projects must be started—and completed).

Do that for *each phase* of the campaign. All six phases.

The Master Calendar

Now, let's translate those six sheets, and their project lists, to a master calendar.

Get yourself a great big calendar. One that starts long before election day and one with date squares large enough for you to pencil in the projects under each day. If you can't find one at the stationers, make your own. Get 10 or 16 large sheets of newsprint or wrapping paper (about three feet by four feet). Starting about two inches down from the top edge, mark out the squares for the days and the weeks of the month—seven squares across and five squares down. Print the month and the year in those top two inches you left, and then number each square with the days of that month. When you have finished that little chore you will have up to a 16-month calendar, 16 sheets—one for each month from the time you ideally start the campaign until you win on election day.

Now, take those six sheets on which you itemized the basic campaign projects for each of the six phases of the campaign and transcribe them to your calendar—day-by-day, month-by-month.

Here's a tip: figure out when the committee will need a certain item—such as the results of the district statistical analysis; or, the first findings of the public opinion poll. Mark those dates on your calendar. Now, compute *the length of time* it should take to complete those projects: 30 days? 60 days? three months?—whatever. Go backward on your calendar from the completion date the number of days it will take to do the project and *mark that day* as the point at which the project must be underway. If it is not started on that day, chances are it will not be completed on time.

Obviously, you cannot possibly know all the problems and last-minute details that may crop up during the campaign. But, you can schedule all of the *basic elements* and all of the *foundation work* that must be done.

When you have finished transferring the items from the detail sheets to the calendar, you will have polished off a 16-months winning campaign. All you and the committee have to do now is put the timetable to work—follow the calendar and see to it that all of the work is done . . . *on time.* It may have seemed a tedious and time-consuming task but it is the best way to stay ahead of all the many details in a political campaign; the only way to get things done in the right way and by the right day.

Double-check Your Calendar

Review the master calendar with the campaign strategy committee.

How does it look? Does it look realistic? Does it look as though it will work? Are there days or weeks where everything is bunched together? *Can you move some things ahead,* or back, to even the load? Are there empty periods? *Can you move certain projects back* to fill that void and also give the folks working on the project more time?

When you have everything just about the way you want it, consider it your *basic campaign timetable.* It can be adjusted, later on. *It's flexible,* especially if you have started early enough to give the campaign time to take unexpected situations in stride.

Just make sure you don't bend the timetable so much it ends up being useless. A timetable is a harsh *taskmaster* but that is just what is needed in a fast-moving campaign.

When the campaign headquarters is opened, *post the calendar on the wall in the chairman's office.* Follow it day-by-day; it is a working document. In the meantime, have it on hand at all strategy committee meetings for ready reference.

A Typical Timetable

Here is a basic timetable for a typical campaign.

Some campaigns—such as those for a school board seat or a city council race—will not require so much detail and so many activities. *Adjust your timetable to fit your needs.*

This timetable is based on the assumption of a *June primary* and a *November general election.* If the primary in your state is held in a different month, or if the final election is held at a different time (as it usually is in off-years, special elections, etc.) compensate accordingly. *But, remember:* if you possibly can, start working on your campaign 10 to 16 months before the big election.

I. THE EXTRA-EARLY PERIOD

This begins 10 to 16 months before election day. In other words, if you are aiming for a June primary, this phase of the campaign should start in March, and no later than September, of the preceding year.

- Call key members of your group together. Hold an organizational meeting.
- Constitute the group as a strategy committee and fill these posts:
    —chairman, co-chairman, finance, research and scheduling chairman. Also, a chairman of the candidate search committee. (If you cannot fill all those spots at the first meeting, set a date for the next meeting and make sure that individuals are lined up for those key jobs by then.)
- Agree on a target—the public office you will try to win.
- Start search for a candidate
- Add to the strategy committee (chairmen of publicity, precinct, legal counsel, and treasurer)
- Legal counsel prepares digest of campaign laws
- Research and precinct chairman start preliminary work on statistical analysis of district (this should be completed six months before primary election)
- Start low-key fund-raising effort (within group and only with selected individuals; raise just enough money at this time to cover cost of incidentals)
- Screen and select candidate(s)
- Get candidate's acceptance and agreement to run
- Scheduling chairman starts obtaining appearances for candidate-to-be including neighborhood coffees
- Start making candidate-to-be better known (as an individual, not as a candidate)
- Establish monitoring (feedback) on candidate's appearances
- Begin basic research operations
    —background on key issues, socio-economic data on district,

opponent's record (if incumbent), etc.
- Hold regular meetings of strategy committee
  —review progress, plan ahead

II. THE RUNNING START

This period covers the six months prior to the candidate's official declaration of intention—or announcement of his candidacy. If you are aiming for a June primary, this phase should begin in November or December of the preceding year. Things start picking up steam during this phase.
- Complete formation of campaign strategy committee
  —all committee chairmen selected and at work
- Complete district statistical analysis
- Make map of priority precincts for regional and area precinct leaders
- Regional and area precinct leaders start building their organizations
- Start the first public opinion poll
  —if this is to be done by volunteers, precinct chairman should recruit and, in cooperation with general campaign chairman and research chairman, hold training sessions for volunteers.
- Make decision as to hiring professional campaign management
  —if funds available and decision affirmative, begin search and selection of agency or individual
- Finance chairman begins drive for campaign pledges and contributions
- Have candidate's campaign photographs taken now
- Complete draft of basic campaign literature
  —at least one brochure on candidate and several flyers (one-pagers) on key issues
- Design basic campaign graphics
  —colors, style, type face, etc.
- Continue and accelerate candidate's public appearances

    —public meetings

    —coffees and neighborhood receptions

- Step up publicity on candidate-to-be
- Headquarters chairman lines up space and negotiates lease
- Make arrangements for liability insurance, etc., on headquarters
- Arrange for headquarters utilities, phones, etc.
- Complete first public opinion poll
- Analyze poll results

    —adjust speeches, campaign literature, etc., to reflect poll

- Get final approval on campaign literature and order first run

    —must be delivered at least two weeks before official start of campaign

- Candidate and public relations chairman meet in backgrounder sessions with key media contacts to sound them out about the candidacy
- Candidate begins to indicate publicly he is thinking of running for office.
- Committee members begin to promote candidacy by word of mouth
- Public relations chairman (or agency) reserves billboards

    —can be done through friendly firm

    —reserved in two "waves"—first wave starting 60 days before primary and second wave starting 30 days before

- If campaign plans to use TV, reserve TV time now
- Finance chairman moves into high gear
- Campaign materials are delivered

    —stationery, pledge cards, sign-up cards

    —candidate's brochure

    —bumper stickers, posters, etc.

- Sign painter is alerted for headquarters signing
- Candidate makes major public speech on issue directly connected with the office, or concerning the shortcomings of the way that office is being conducted (not an attack on the incumbent)
- *Candidate announces he intends to run for office*

FORMAL CAMPAIGN BEGINS NOW
(Election Day minus 60)

(The formal campaign starts about 60 days before election day. If we are talking about a June primary, the formal campaign should begin on about April 1. This is flexible. In some states candidates must declare their intention to run earlier than April 1. *Check your state manual or your state election code.* Also, be sure to pick a date for the candidate's formal announcement that is calculated to generate *maximum publicity.* Also, if there is any unusual twist or setting that can be used to increase public interest in announcement, use it.)

III. THE GRAND OPENING!

This period covers the first 30 days of the 60 days remaining before election day.

- Candidate officially declares he is running for office
- Kick off rally for supporters and volunteers
- Candidate files papers, holds first press conference
- Grand opening of central headquarters (open house rally)
- Signs go up at headquarters
- First wave of billboards up (60-day run, through primary day)
- First wave of bumper stickers go on
- Public relations chairman distributes candidate press kit to key media contacts
- Precinct chairman and assistants accelerate precinct work
  - Registration drive (continue until registration closes)
  - begin expanded precinct effort (esp. in priority precincts)
- Accelerate candidate's public activities
  - tour safe (best) areas *now,* generate show of support
  - maintain steady schedule of "coffees"
  - start tour of outlying communities and shopping centers
- Step-up speech schedule
  - start hitting at key issues (hard, and harder)
- Start second public opinion survey
- Hold first ($25 or $50) fund-raiser

- Begin regular announcements and news releases on
  - appointments of chairmen
  - formation of special committees
  - early endorsements
- Start posting signs and cards in rural areas

IV. THE "BIG SELL" STARTS

This period covers the first 15 days of the 30 days remaining before the primary election. In a primary campaign climaxing in June, this phase should start on about May 1. Candidate and committee starts going all-out NOW!

- Begin 50 percent TV and radio ad schedule
- Begin initial (small space) newspaper campaign
- Second wave of billboards go up (30-day run, through primary)
- Candidate starts making at least one major issue speech a week
  - amplifies that speech at subsequent appearances during week
  - public relations chairman services press with advance texts
  - public relations chairman provides follow-up coverage of speech to media (especially weekly newspaper and smaller radio stations)
- Open outlying community headquarters on programmed schedule to sustain publicity and interest (rallies and open houses)
- Results of second public opinion survey in and analyzed
- First wave f lawn (yard) cards go up
- Direct mail promotion (number one) to all eligible primary voters
- Candidate adjusts speech material and news releases to reflect findings of second public opinion poll
- If necessary, make adjustments in TV and radio commercials to reflect latest public opinion poll
- Prepare newspaper ads (large space) to run during final weeks
- Make final check and beef up weak spots in precinct operation

- Keep up steady flow of public announcement on
  —more committee appointments
  —more endorsement by key groups
  —more new special committees
- Begin building special Election Day task groups
  —cars and drivers to take voters to polls
  —baby-sitters, etc.
- Begin recruitment of volunteers for victory squads

V. THE FAST CLOSE

This is the home stretch! Everything and everybody in the campaign is going full tilt and flat out for the final 15 days. In a June primary contest, this phase starts on about May 20.

- Start full ad schedule on TV
- Start full ad schedule on radio
- Step up telephone campaign to solicit votes for candidate
- Second wave of bumper stickers goes on
- Second wave of lawn (and yard) cards go up
- Family night ($10) fund-raiser(s)
- Candidate makes major speech and presents U.V.P.
- U.V.P. mailer to all citizens eligible to vote in primary
- Candidate zeroes in on marginal precincts and works major shopping centers in those areas.
- Final pep rally for precinct workers and other volunteers and supporters (public invited)
- Precinct workers begin final canvass
  —literature hand out
  —check on those who need absentee ballots or election assistance
- Victory squads recruited and trained and assigned
- Legal counsel briefs lawyers task force to assist poll watchers
- Final press conference for candidate
- Final (big) newspaper ads run
  —combination repeat of U.V.P. (or blast on key issues) and large scale listing of endorsements and supporters

VI. ELECTION DAY!

Everybody out to the polls!
And, then to the precincts to work for victory.
(For a detailed, hour-by-hour schedule of election day action, see Chapter Thirteen, *"All Out For Election Day!"*)

CHAPTER THIRTEEN

All Out For Election Day!

*"All your efforts and those of your many volunteer workers
. . . stand or fall on your ability to get out the vote on Election
Day."*

COPE Handbook *

This is it. The big day! The day you and your co-workers have
been aiming for and building toward.

You have canvassed the voters. You have helped to register the
unregistered and distributed the candidate's literature. You know
the names and addresses of all your sure votes. You have recruited
the baby-sitters and the cars and drivers for those who will need
assistance.

And now the time has come: Election day!

Your job is to deliver your votes. To get each and every one
of those voters to the polls; to carry your precinct and your district
for your candidate.

Remember: elections have been, and will be, won or lost by one
vote per precinct. *Don't quit until every one of your voters has been
to the polls and cast a vote for your candidate!*

---

* "How to Win, Handbook for Political Education", AFL-CIO Committee
on Political Education.

Election Day Precinct Headquarters

Election day should not be a hit-and-miss affair. Make sure your efforts are fully coordinated so that *all* the details are covered and *all* the work is done—*thoroughly and on time.*

Establish an election-day central, a field headquarters to be the focal point of your all-out efforts. Locate this base of operations near—but not next to—the polling place in your precinct. Perhaps one of your blockworkers or volunteers lives near the polls and will offer the use of his, or her, home.

A two-car garage makes a good election-day headquarters. Be sure there is plenty of heat and light. Otherwise, a dining room or a family room or recreation room will do just fine.

Your election-day central should be equipped with
  —a *large map of your precinct* (posted on a wall so that your volunteers can have easy access to it)
  —the *latest registration index of voters* in your precinct (this, too, should be posted in a prominent place)
  —several *work tables and chairs* along one side of the room
  —an *alphabetical card file* of all those voters in your precinct who are *definitely for your candidate.*
  —a *shoe box* labelled "Have Voted"
  —a supply of one-page *"Election Day Instructions"*
  —a supply of *doorknob hangers* or "Please Vote" reminders
  —a supply of *pencils, scratch pads and rubberbands,* and
  —an *election day kit* for each block in the precinct.

Election Day Kits

On the day before the election, the precinct captain and the two or three persons who have volunteered to serve as headquarters staff should make up an *election day kit* for each and every block in the precinct. Each kit should include:
  —an *"Election Day Instructions"* memo
  —a supply of *doorknob hangers*
  —a *pencil and note pad*

—(if necessary) a mimeographed sheet of pertinent information on *what poll checkers can and cannot do* (excerpted from the *state election code),* and

—a rubberbanded *set of file cards* with the name and address of each and every one of *your* voters in that block.

All of those materials should be placed into a large manila envelope with the number or description of the block printed on the front of the envelope. The envelopes should then be filed, in proper order, in a cut-down carton, arranged so that the block number can be readily seen.

TYPICAL ELECTION DAY
INSTRUCTION MEMO

Precinct Headquarters: Block # _____
    (address)
_____

    (phone number)
_____

ELECTION DAY INSTRUCTIONS
For Blockworkers
Message from the candidate:

"You and I have been working on this campaign for many long months. Together we have worked the precincts to find and register new voters. We have contacted the voters on behalf of our campaign and we have walked or phoned the blocks to find our SURE votes. All this and more we have done to gain the victory. *But, all of our effort will have been wasted if we fail to deliver OUR vote at the polls . . . TODAY!*

"Please don't quit until each and every one of our voters has been to the polls! And, thanks—thanks from all of us."

            /s/   (candidate's signature)
_____

1. CHECK YOUR BLOCKWORKER'S KIT

    It contains your set of voter cards—one card for each SURE voter in your block. Your job is to make sure that every one votes TODAY.

2. CHECK THE VOTER LIST

    Report to your precinct headquarters no later than 1 p.m. The voter list for your precinct will be posted there. The names of those voters on your block WHO HAVE ALREADY VOTED will have been checked off. As more "Have Voted" names are received from the polls, these will be checked off, too. CHECK THE VOTER LIST FREQUENTLY. *Keep tabs on who in your block has not yet voted.*

3. CHECK YOUR VOTER CARDS

Pull the cards on those voters *who have already voted*. Keep these cards in order (by street and number), put a rubberband around them and put them back in your manila envelope. (Repeat this process each time you check the precinct voter list)

4. CONTACT THOSE WHO HAVE NOT VOTED

Based on the "HAVE NOT VOTED" cards, personally contact each and every person who has yet to vote. Urge them to vote, offer assistance. Emphasize that one vote IS important and *their* one vote could make the difference.

5. IF THE VOTER IS NOT HOME . . .

Leave a doorknob hanger (several have been placed in your kit). If the citizen has not voted by 5:30 or 6 p.m., *contact his home again*.

DON'T QUIT until each and every *sure* voter has been to the polls. A promise to vote is NOT a vote. Only when a name has been crossed off the voter list at precinct headquarters should you transfer that card to your "Have Voted" pile.

6. AFTER THE POLLS CLOSE . . .

. . . or, when all your voters have voted, return to the precinct headquarters. *Turn in your kit.* If you are needed to help at headquarters or in another block, please help.

> AND, DON'T FORGET! VICTORY POT LUCK! EIGHT O'CLOCK AT ＿＿＿＿＿＿. BRING THE FAMILY. WATCH THE VOTE RETURNS WITH THE REST OF YOUR WINNING TEAM!

(Note: mimeograph enough of these instruction sheets to have one for each blockworker's kit, plus a small over-supply for headquarters use and for last-minute volunteers.)

Briefing Session

The election-day headquarters should be set up on the afternoon before election day. At that time make sure that all materials and supplies are in order, on hand, and in place.

Call a briefing session for *election eve*. Make sure that all volunteers who have election day assignments are present at that briefing and, at that time, make sure that all will be on hand at the appointed time on election day. This includes headquarters personnel, blockworkers, victory squad members and those who have special assignments such as transportation, baby-sitting, poll checking, messenger service, etc.

Hold your election eve briefing at the election-day central so that all the workers will be able to familiarize themselves with the headquarters location and facilities.

Go over the election day details step-by-step, hour by hour. Preview the entire operation so that everyone will get the complete picture.

Basically, your election day effort will comprise these operations:

—*precinct headquarters* (directed by the precinct captain with the assistance of two or three volunteers to handle clerical duties, etc.)

—*blockworkers* (ideally one to each and every block in the precinct)

—*victory squad*

—*poll checking*

—*messengers* (whose job is to relay information between the poll checkers and the precinct headquarters; teenagers can do a great job on this detail)

—*poll watching*

—*transportation* (providing cars and drivers for voters who have requested such assistance) and

—*baby-sitters* (for those voters who need such a service).

Review all of this at your briefing session. Encourage questions and try to answer all of them. Distribute the blockworker kits and review the purpose and use of each item in the kit. Assign the hours of duty to your drivers and your baby sitters.

Generate a feeling of oneness, a sense of enthusiasm, and a desire for victory. *Close your briefing session with prayer*—not a prayer for victory but, more importantly, a prayer that all will conduct themselves as Christians, and *that The Lord's will be done*—win or lose.

Election Day

Election-day morning will seem rather slow—almost anti-climactic. Your workers will be all geared-up, ready to go, and yet at the start of the day there will seem to be little to do: the real, all-out effort starts after lunch. Take advantage of this early lull to make sure that all of your *co-workers go and vote.* Get that out of the way early. Sometimes precinct workers become so involved in getting others out to vote that they forget to vote themselves. *Don't let that happen!* Those votes are important.

Election-day morning is also a good time for the transportation detail to take their early bird voters to the polls. And, it is also a good time to babysit for busy housewives who want to vote early. If as much of this is completed as possible during the morning hours (from eight o'clock until noon) there will be less pressure during the hectic hours at the close of election day.

The full-scale precinct headquarters operation should get underway right after lunch—*and no later than one o'clock.*

Starting at that time, the poll checker can supply the election-day precinct headquarters with the first batch of cards on those friendly voters who cast their ballots during the morning hours (and also the names of those who voted by *absentee ballot*—names that should be available from the election board at the polling place).Those names can be pulled from the card file and deposited in the "Have Voted" box. In that way, you can start your operations with a "clean" file—containing only the cards on those of your voters who have *not yet* voted.

Those cards—the ones in the master file as of one o'clock—are your targets. By the time the polls close every one of those cards should have been transferred from the files to the "Have Voted" box. When that is accomplished you will know you have had a *one hundred percent turn-out* of all *your* voters in the precinct!

Checking The Polls

There is only one sure way to find out who has and has not voted in your precinct. That is to keep a constant check on your precinct polling place.

Most states require the election board officials to post a copy of the voter index (registration list) outside the entrance to the

polling place and to mark off—at regular intervals—the names of
those voters who have cast ballots. This is done by drawing a line
through the name of the voter as it appears on the posted list.
These check-offs are usually done at least once each hour, up to
the final hours of voting. The names of the last-minute voters are
checked off *after* the polls have closed and before the vote tally
is started.

Assign a poll checker to your precinct polling place. This person
should be pleasant but also have the determination to get the job
done. He, or she, should be equipped with

—a set of 3″ x 5″ *file cards*—each card bearing the name of
   a registered resident of the precinct who is *for* your candidate
   (these cards should be in alphabetical order)
—a supply of *rubber bands*
—a supply of standard-size (4″ x 9½″) *envelopes* marked "Have
   Voted"
—a copy of those sections of the *state elections code* that pertain
   to poll checking, and
—a *letter of authorization,* signed by the candidate or the campaign chairman, stating that the bearer has been appointed
   poll checker for that precinct.

The first thing the poll checker should do, upon arriving at the
polling place, is to introduce himself, or herself, to the members
of the precinct election board. If the checker lives in the precinct,
he or she probably will know one or two of the ladies on the
board. In fact, if the candidate's committee has done its job properly, at least one member of the board will be a committee recruit.

It is the poll checker's job to *keep tabs on the posted* voter list
and to check it immediately *each time an election official posts
the names of those who cast their ballots* during the preceding
interval.

As the poll checker goes down the list of voters, he pulls from
his files the cards of those friendly voters who have cast their ballot
and places them in one of the "Have Voted" envelopes. When
he, or she, has completed that check of the voter list, he arranges
the "Have Voted" cards alphabetically, puts a rubber band around
them, places them in the envelope ready for *delivery to the precinct
headquarters.*

At regular intervals—once every hour starting at 1 p.m. and at least twice each hour starting at 5 p.m.—a *precinct messenger* should contact the poll checker, pick up the "Have Voted" envelope and deliver it *immediately* to the precinct headquarters. This delivery system continues until every friendly voter in the precinct has cast a ballot or until the polls are closed.

During the closing (and often hectic) hours at the polls (or, if your state does not require the posting and checking of a voter list), the poll checker should stand *inside* the polling place near enough to the election board tables *to hear the voters names as they sign-in and are read off.* Be sure not to stand in the flow of traffic or to interrupt the voting process in any way. If one of the election officials challenges the poll checker, the checker should pleasantly but firmly go over the excerpts from the election codes pertaining to the legality of poll checking. It is very unusual that there is any problem in that regard.

The poll checker remains at the polls until the polls are closed and the last voter has cast a ballot. Then the checker returns to the precinct headquarters and turns in any left-over materials or supplies.

Poll Watchers

Don't confuse the poll *checker* with the poll *watcher.* The duty of the poll checker is to keep tabs on those citizens who have voted and to help deliver the votes for your candidate. The duties of the poll watcher are entirely different: *to make sure that no illegal voting or election fraud takes place at the polls.*

Poll watching is seldom necessary in rural or suburban areas where most folks know each other and the voting habits are fairly well established. But poll watching can be essential in those urban and suburban areas that have a high population turn-over and are the natural habitat of the big political machine.

It is best to assign the job of poll watching to a man; preferably a husky man, and preferably an attorney. There is less likelihood of such an individual being intimidated or ignored.

Remember that house-to-house canvass your workers made earlier in the campaign? It provided you with the latest information on who lives at what address, who has died, who has moved away, or who has moved in. From that data you know who is, and is not, eligible to vote in your precinct. Because you have been doing your job, that information has been noted on the cards in your precinct file.

(Back in Chapter Ten—*"The Winning Place"*—the importance of keeping those precinct card files up-to-date was detailed. You are now in a position to prove that point, if you have to.)

The poll watcher for your candidate should be at the polling place from the time it opens until the votes are tallied. Because of the long day involved, you probably should assign two persons to the job, so that they can spell each other.

Those who are assigned as poll watchers should have with them:
   —a *letter of authorization* (stating that they are the official poll watchers at the precinct for the candidate or party)
   —a copy of the voter index for the precinct *with the names of the non-eligible voters checked in red* (or a typed list of those who are not eligible to vote in the precinct—*and why;* individuals whose names may appear on the list of voters but who are not eligible to vote because they are deceased, or no longer reside in the precinct, or because there is no such address in the precinct or the address is a vacant lot, etc.)
   Make sure this information is correct. Check it and recheck it before giving it to the poll watcher!
   —a copy (or excerpts) of the *state election code* pertaining to the provisions for and the rights of poll watchers.

Upon arrival at the polls, the poll watcher should introduce himself to the members of the precinct election board. He then stations himself inside the polling place—in a corner to the side so that he does not interfere with the voting process.

By studying the list of potential challenges, the poll watcher can familiarize himself with the names in question and be ready to raise a challenge quickly if someone tries to vote under one of those names. If such fraud is attempted it will often occur *during the final hours of voting* when the polling place is crowded and the election officials are busy attending to their regular duties.

When the need to challenge arises, the poll watcher should step forward quickly and say to the election board official, in a quiet but firm voice: "Pardon me, I challenge that voter." Then he should state the basis for the challenge: "Mr. _____ died three years ago", or "Mrs. _____ moved from that address six months ago, on _____ (exact date) _____", or "_____ (address) _____ is a vacant lot".

The election official will probably query the would-be-voter and ask for some identification or proof of residency. The would-be-voter may (a.) make a hasty exit or (b.) try to bluff his way through hoping that the official's desire to keep the line of voters moving will cause her to waive the challenge. In that event, the poll watcher should request the election official to call the county clerk for advice or assistance and inform the official, pleasantly but firmly, that otherwise he will file a formal charge of fraud with the county prosecutor.

At that point the election board official may ask the challenged voter to stand aside and wait while she calls the county clerk's office so that others may vote. The poll watcher may also want to call his campaign headquarters to seek assistance from one of the attorneys on hand there to help in such situations (see *"Legal Counsel"*, Chapter Eight).

In all of this the poll watcher should never get obnoxious, or threatening, or cause any undue disturbance. He should be firm, determined, but as quiet as possible—and courteous. As long as he conducts himself properly, *he is well within the law;* doing his job to protect the sanctity of the ballot box and the validity of the legitimate votes.

All this may seem a lot of effort just to prevent one illegal vote. But remember: that one vote is important. *If it were not, someone would not have gone to such great lengths to try and get it cast.* Then, too, by making it clear that your committee is prepared to challenge voter fraud *you may scare off others* who had intended to do the same thing.

Meanwhile, Back at Headquarters . . .

When the messenger delivers the "Have Voted" envelope from the checker at the polling place, those names are *crossed off the voter index* (registration list), *the cards are pulled from the master file and placed into* the headquarters *"Have Voted" box.* This procedure is followed each time the messenger brings new cards back from the polls and continues until all the cards in the master file have been transferred to the "Have Voted" box. Make sure that the cards in the "Have Voted" box are kept in *alphabetical order,* ready for use; you may have to take a quick double-check later on in the day.

At regular intervals the blockworkers will be checking back to see which of their voters has yet to cast a ballot. Make sure the voter index is kept up-to-the-minute. If you have the time, and help, you might want to file the "Have Voted" cards in separate boxes, *by block;* that would be a real help to the blockworkers. If you do file the "Have Voted" cards by block, use those cards returned by the poll checker for that purpose. Do not use the cards from the master file.

Victory Squads

Sometimes, no matter how hard your precinct captains try, there are blocks without blockworkers; neighborhoods where your get-out-the-vote efforts are weak and need help.

That's where the victory squads come in!

These are *special election day forces* that can be deployed to cover your weak spots and to help make sure that your maximum vote is delivered. The victory squads are the reserve forces for your precinct organization.

How do you build the victory squad?

Basically, from those individuals who want to help your candidate but cannot get involved in the campaign over a prolonged period of time. Thus, they volunteer to work on election day. *Some volunteer, others are recruited from a variety of sources:*

—from the ranks of executives, junior executives, management and middle management personnel at local offices and factories (young executives from insurance and stock brokerage and investment firms are prime prospects because of their training and ability to meet the public, sell themselves, etc.)

—through chambers of commerce, or trade and professional and service organizations (including women's groups and auxiliaries), and

—from church congregations, Bible classes, men's and women's clubs and young people's groups in the churches, and on the college and junior college campuses.

If your precinct organization has been functioning properly, *long before election day* the precinct captains advised their area coordinators of the victory squad help that would be needed in their precincts. The area coordinators, in turn, advised the campaign headquarters (the campaign precinct chairman and victory squad director) of their total requirements. Thus, several weeks before election day, headquarters should have a good idea of the number of victory squad recruits that will be needed.

How do you use the victory squad? (And, after recruiting these volunteers, make sure you do!)

The victory squad members are asked to report to campaign headquarters early on the afternoon of election day—no later than two o'clock. They are directed, from there, to *the precinct headquarters* to which they have been assigned. From that point on, they work *under the direction of the precinct captain* who gives them their election day kit, their instructions, and their get-out-your-vote assignments.

Getting Out Your Vote

The job, of course, is to get out every one of *your* votes. To make sure that each and every registered voter who has indicated a preference for your candidate casts a ballot.

It's a personal, door-to-door or phone campaign and if you and your co-workers in the precinct have done the job, someone from your committee has knocked on those doors before. That early contact will come in handy today—it will pay dividends in getting out your vote.

A good blockworker knows his, or her, block; knows the voters in the block; knows them by name if not by sight. A good block-worker knows the voters who support the candidate; knows what time of the day they will probably vote (on the way to work, during the lunch hour, after work—or, by absentee ballot). If it is necessary for the blockworker to call at a home to remind the voter to go to the polls, it will be like a visit from a friend or a neighbor.

To sum it up: a good blockworker should have no problem at all in delivering one hundred percent of the friendly vote in his or her block. Election day duties are, primarily, a matter of making sure that no last-minute hitches arise to keep one of the voters from the polls and to provide any service (transportation or baby sitting) should the need suddenly develop.

So, the good blockworker picks up the kit for his block, keeps tabs on his votes, makes a house call here and there to remind a lagging voter to get to the polls, and—perhaps—spends a few moments talking to someone on the block who was on the fence and might just be convinced that your candidate is for sure the one to elect.

On the other hand, if your precinct is not well-organized, and you must rely on *last-minute volunteers* to get out your vote, the election-day work takes on an added dimension. The volunteer will be *a stranger at the door or on the phone*—an unknown quantity to the voter. Thus, care must be taken to establish a *pleasant and friendly situation* each time a voter call is made (hopefully, you will have at least located *your* voters in the precinct).

Here are a few *tips to help the volunteer* election day worker do the best job for your candidate:

Ring the doorbell or knock on the door, then step back several steps, so that you do not present a threat to the person who opens the door. When the door opens, *smile and say:*

"How do you do. My name is _____ (name) _____. I'm a volunteer for _____ (name of candidate) _____ who is running for _____ (office) _____ on the _____ (name of party) _____ ticket."

(Since the voter has previously indicated, to one of the campaign canvassers, that he or she favors your candidate your opening should evoke an agreeable response. Give the person an opportunity to reply. *Then continue.*)

"This is election day, of course, and we would just like to remind you (and your husband or wife, etc). to be sure to vote." *Pause.*

(The voter will no doubt respond, "Oh, yes. We're going to vote as soon as my husband (or wife) gets home from work (or whatever).")

The volunteer should *smile and say:* "That's great. Is there any service we can provide? Will you need a baby sitter to stay here while you go to the polls? Could we send a car and driver?"

(Or, suppose the homeowner replies to the reminder to vote, "Yes, I know it's election day but my husband is out of town" or "I just can't leave because the car won't work". The volunteer *immediately offers assistance:* "We'll be glad to have a sitter come over" or "We'll send a car and driver for you—would 30 minutes from now be all right?")

Whatever—whether the voter assures the volunteer that he or she will be going to the polls, or arrangements are made for a baby-sitter or car and driver—the volunteer should close the conversation with a *friendly goodbye:*

"Thank you very much for your support. We're sure counting on your vote. Incidentally, your polling place is at _____ (address) _____. Good afternoon!"

If a request for voter service was made, the volunteer should immediately relay this information to the precinct election central. Someone at the headquarters should (a.) *call the voter* to confirm that a baby sitter (or car and driver) will be there in ____ minutes and then (b.) *dispatch whatever service was requested* so that it arrives at the voter's home at the appointed time.

Or, By Phone

The ideal way to cover your precincts and get out your vote is by having your workers go door-to-door, house-to-house. Experience has shown that is the best way to motivate the voter: he figures if you can take the time to come to him, the least he can do is take the time to go the polls.

However, it is not always possible to have sufficient time and manpower to cover each friendly house with a personal, in person, call. Thus, you must use the telephone—the next best way to get out the vote.

Remember how we stressed the importance of keeping those voter card files up-to-date? And how important it was to write the phone numbers on each card? Well, now is the time when all that work pays off! The voter cards are in order and each card has the correct phone number. The election-day phone workers can go through the cards in a hurry, without having to stop and wrestle with the phonebook.

Basically, the technique for using the phone to get out your vote is the same as if the workers were going house-to-house:

"Hello, _____ (name of voter) _____. This is _____ (worker's name) _____. I'm calling from _____ (name of candidate or party) headquarters. We'd like to remind you that today is election day." (Pause)

(The voter will probably respond, "Yes, we just got back from voting" or "Yes, we're going down to vote right after dinner" or "When my husband gets home" etc.)

"That's great. Your vote is important." If the voter has not yet voted be sure to ask, "Is there any service we can perform—do you need a baby sitter? Or, a car to drive you to the polls?"

Of course, if the voter responds that such help would be appreciated the worker makes arrangements to provide that service.

Be sure to close with a friendly good-bye and—if the voter has not yet gone to the polls—a reminder to "Please don't forget to vote, we're counting on you".

Nobody Home

If the blockworker, or the volunteer, finds no one home, make sure they put a *doorknob hanger on the front door*. This will let the voter know you called while he was out, and will remind him to go to the polls. Be sure the correct address of the polling place is printed or written on the hanger, along with a reminder that the polls close at _____p.m. If the blockworker knows the folks in the house, he or she should autograph the card, to lend a personal touch. They might even add a note, such as "Hi, Joe! Don't forget to vote for _____ (name of candidate) _____!"

If, by 5:30 or 6 p.m., the voter has still not gone to the polls, *call on the phone or go back and try again.* Maybe they are home by now. If so, urge them to vote. If not, keep trying until the polls are closed. *Don't quit.* That one vote—or those two votes—could make the difference!

Doorknob Hangers

The doorknob hanger is a printed reminder ("Please vote!") that is slipped around the doorknob of the front door if the voter is not home.

Usually, these hangers are supplied by the campaign headquarters. They are die-cut cards with a hole or a slot that goes around the doorknob and are long enough for a message printed in the space below the place for the doorknob. However, if your campaign cannot afford the cost of these special printing jobs, *make your own doorknob hanger.* Here's how:

Use a large file card (4″ x 5″). Print or write a friendly vote reminder and the address of the polling place on the face of the card. Use a felt pen, if possible. On the reverse side of the card, scribble a note that the polls close at _____ p.m., and add "We'd sure appreciate your vote for _____ (name of candidate) _____!"

Punch a hole in the upper corner of the card. Slip one end (or loop) of a rubberband through the hole and pull it through halfway. Then, put the two loops together and slip them around the doorknob. *Voila!* A handy-dandy, inexpensive and personalized doorknob hanger! It should look something like this:

HI! SORRY WE MISSED YOU!!

JUST DROPPED BY TO REMIND YOU THAT THIS

IS ELECTION DAY AND YOUR POLLING PLACE IS

_____

_____

Front side of your handy-dandy, home-made doorknob hanger. Reverse side of card should state: "Don't forget, the polls close at _____ p.m. AND, PLEASE DON'T FORGET TO VOTE FOR _____ (name of candidate) for _____ _____ (office)!" Blockworker should then sign name for personal touch.

Literature Tables

Some states permit candidate committees to place literature tables in the vicinity of the polling place. If you decide to use this device, be sure to place your card table *the required distance away from the polling place*—plus ten feet, just to be safe. Tape a "Voter Information" sign to the *front edge* of the table. Be sure to have plenty of your *candidate's literature* on hand; pick that piece that gives the best sales pitch in the shortest reading time.

Make sure that

—your literature table is located and manned *in complete compliance* with the law, and

—those volunteers who staff the table are *pleasant, courteous, and not overly-eager or obnoxious*.

Properly handled, the literature table is an added touch that can produce some *bonus votes* from "undecided" voters.

After The Polls Close

When your "get out the vote" work is done, and when the polls are closed, return your kit to precinct headquarters. The materials can be used for future work. Blockworkers who complete their tasks early should report to the precinct headquarters to see if they can help—either in the headquarters or in those blocks where there are still friendly voters to be gotten to the polls.

Most campaigns hold open house at headquarters on election night so that the workers and their friends can gather together to watch the returns come in. Or, perhaps your group could plan a pot luck dinner at the church, or someone's home, so that all the workers in your precinct (and their families) can enjoy the evening together.

Whatever, you deserve a few hours to celebrate the victory you helped achieved.

But, don't pat yourself on the back too long. There is still a lot of work to be done! *There sure is!!*

In its "Handbook for Political Education", COPE—the AFL-CIO's Committee on Political Education, gives this advice to its members:

"There's a special pleasure that comes the day after the election, when you pick up the morning paper and see in cold print the reports of a victory you helped fashion.

"And there's a special determination to do better the next time, if you lose.

"But, win or lose, you must now get to work on the next campaign.

"That's right!

"The time to begin political organization for the next election is the day after the last one."

That's just the way it is for most political organizations. There is no such thing as an off-election year or a non-working time; they are at it constantly. And, if just plain citizens are going to be any kind of a match for such organized and well-financed special interest machines, you must also be active on a regular basis.

Besides, as Christians we have more than just "political knitting" to attend to.

The General Elections

Let's say that your work and effort has won the primary for your candidate. In the language of the sports world, the primary was only the play-offs—*the general election is the super bowl!*

So, that means the next big job starts right now—working to win the general election in November. To get your candidate in office.

That means you all get right to work. The candidate keeps campaigning, the subcommittees keep working and building, and the precinct organizations keep digging away—registering new voters, selling more voters on the candidate, perfecting its campaign and election day techniques.

The big difference, now, is that all registered voters—*in both parties and not just your party*—can vote for your candidate come November. Thus, from here on out you work to keep the votes you won in the primary and add enough new votes to carry the precinct in the general. Your targets include:

—those *members of your party* who may have voted for your primary opponent

—the *independent voters* in your precinct

—those *members of the other party* who can be "sold" on your candidate, and

—the *new voters* who are now eligible to register and vote in November because they have fulfilled the requirements of residency or voting age.

If your party is on the short end of the registration ratio in your district (or precinct) you obviously have to get voters from the other party to cross party lines and vote for your candidate. Get started. Sell them on the basis of principles and performance. Figure out how many cross-over voters you need to win the election, and go get 'em!

Work your precincts as you did in the primary campaign. Canvass the voters, register the friendly voters, make your candidate literature drops, do your pre-election vote count, service those who need absentee ballots, check on those who may need baby-sitters and transportation.

It's a matter of doing what you did to win the primary election— *but doing more of it and doing it even better.*

Or, After November

Even if you and your co-workers have just won the November (general) election, there are still great things to be done.

For one thing, now is the time to really start on those Christian service projects in your precincts or district. (Remember Chapter Twelve, *"Do Thou Likewise"*?) Put the organization you built during the campaign to work helping others. Start Bible study groups in the precincts. Go out from there. Never was the need greater for Christian love and Good Samaritans. Not just in far-off lands—*but right here at home,* right in your own precinct, your own town, your own county.

You are needed! Faith without works is dead—but works without faith can be deadly. Don't let petticlerks and little Caesars be about the work Christians should be doing. *Put God's love into action.* That, after all, is what effective citizen action is all about.

Elections are important. Electing Christ-centered men and women to public office is vitally important. But, sharing God's love and God's blessings with others in need—not just talking Christianity *but living Christian service*—that is the really important task.

Remember Jake Arvey and those old-time political benefactors? "If Jake Arvey and his machine could do so much in the pursuit of political power, how much more should we do in the practice of Christian love?"

For as much as you do these things unto the least, you do them unto Me.

Go, and do likewise! That is really the essense of Christian citizenship . . . *it is the more excellent way!*

APPENDIX

I. The Care And Keeping Of A Campaign Headquarters

Give your campaign headquarters the planning and attention it deserves. A good headquarters operation can give the campaign a lift. A headquarters that is dull, drab and disorganized will have a negative effect on the entire campaign.

Picking a Site

This is important.

Make sure the headquarters is located in a safe area of town. A headquarters in a rundown section will make it more difficult to recruit volunteer workers; especially if you expect them to work in the late afternoon and evening (after dark).

Be sure the headquarters location is convenient:

—*plenty of parking* next to or close to the office, and

—easy access to *public transportation.*

It is not necessary to locate your headquarters "right in the middle" of downtown, but try to find one fairly close to the center of things. It will help gain more visibility for the candidate and the campaign.

Your headquarters need not be fancy, but it should be safe. Make sure it is not a fire-trap and that it has good light, heat, and ventilation.

Size & Layout

A vacant store makes the ideal campaign headquarters. Sometimes an old home will do, provided it is large enough and has several big rooms for work areas.

The headquarters should have several rooms (private or semi-private) for offices plus a reception area and a good-sized work space. The candidate, the campaign chairman and manager should have *private offices* so that they can make phone calls, hold small meetings, and be alone to think and plan.

Many campaign headquarters combine the reception and work areas; *that is a mistake.* It adds to the confusion, is distracting to the volunteer workers, and often gives the impression of a disorganized (chaotic) campaign. The work area should be located, and arranged, so that it can be transformed into a meeting space during the evening hours. In the latter days of the campaign, there will be meetings in the headquarters several nights a week (precinct meetings, finance sessions, etc.).

Obviously the headquarters must have *restroom facilities* for both men and women.

Try to find a headquarters that provides plenty of *shelf space* for office supplies and campaign materials. If possible, get a headquarters with a back door so that receiving and shipping supplies and materials can be done without traipsing back and forth through the reception area or work space.

Rent

The headquarters chairman, and/or the general chairman, should check with friendly realtors. No doubt several support the candidate and would be glad to help find the best headquarters facility.

You might even find a friendly landlord or realtor who will let you have a good location *without charge*—or at a reduced rent (just enough to cover taxes, insurance, etc.). Usually this can be done if you agree to move should the place be rented. There is a risk to that, of course; you will have to weigh the possibility of having to move during the campaign.

Do not let the offer of no or low rent cause you to take a location without adequate parking or one that is not large enough to accommodate all the headquarters activities that must take place during the campaign.

Insurance

The very first thing you should do—after you have found your headquarters location—*is to take out insurance.* Before you allow one piece of furniture to be moved into the building, before you permit one volunteer to step foot in the place—take out liability insurance.

The cost is small but the protection is great!

There should be at least one insurance agent or broker in your campaign ranks; get him to take care of this liability insurance policy for the committee.

In some states the policy you want is known as "Owners, Landlords, and Tenants" liability insurance. Whatever it is in your state, be sure your committee is covered. You can take out a short-term policy for the duration of the campaign, one that can be cancelled after the election, as soon as the headquarters is vacated.

Safety & Security

Ask the local fire department to inspect the premises. Are there enough *fire exits*? How many *fire extinguishers* are needed? Where should they be placed? Are there any hazardous conditions in the headquarters? How can they be eliminated? All those things should be taken care of *before* the headquarters is opened.

Make sure there are plenty of wastepaper baskets or trash cans and that all waste is put into firetight containers. Do not let waste papers and other trash pile up on the floors; that is a fire hazard and an invitation to other types of accidents.

Be sure that the locks on all the doors and windows are secure and in good working order. Who occupied the building before your committee? Do they still have keys or do you have all the keys to all the doors? Better yet, can you have the locks changed and new keys made?

If possible have at least one filing cabinet that is (a) fireproof and (b) theftproof. All confidential campaign materials and all campaign contributions (cash and checks and financial records) should be kept in those locked files whenever they are on the premises. All campaign funds should be banked daily; only a small amount of (petty) cash should be kept at the headquarters.

Decorating The Headquarters

The headquarters should do a "sales job" for your candidate. Make it bright and attractive.

Use large signs and bright colors. Appealing colors. Keep the headquarters clean, and light and cheerful. This will help lend an air of victory and enthusiasm to the campaign.

Outside: use big signs along the front and sides of the building. If there is a billboard location on or near the building, or in or near the parking lot, post one of the candidate's billboards in that spot; it will be a good morale builder for the volunteers.

Use strong, clean colors for your headquarter signs. If you have selected campaign colors (for brochures, billboards, bumper stickers, etc.) use them; make the cumulative impact of repetition work for you.

Keep the outside grounds (and parking lot) clean. Assign some of the teenagers to that chore.

Inside: if your headquarters has display windows (as in a retail store or supermarket, etc.) *put those windows to work.*

Use large *photos* of the candidate, colored streamers and back-drops, artistic arrangements of *campaign materials,* a *large chart* pin-pointing the candidate's stand on the key issues—large blow-ups of favorable articles or pictures from the local press. Make the windows "sell" for you; keep them interesting, colorful. And, change them occasionally to draw public attention.

If the interior is dull and drab and needs painting, check with the landlord. Get his permission to redecorate. You can supply the manpower. Will he pay for the paint? Do this *before* you move in. Use bright, cheerful, light colors.

In the *reception area* make good use of campaign posters and other campaign materials (lawn cards, large photographs of the candidate, arrangements of campaign literature, bumper stickers, etc.). Display the American flag, prominently. Use one wall for a map or maps of the district. Make up some posters highlighting the candidate's stand on *key issues,* or listing the important points about his background.

If there is a *campaign slogan,* have this painted on a large banner and hang the banner from the ceiling, or along one wall.

Decorations can "telegraph" your message to the voters,—those who pass by and those who drop in. Decorations can lift the spirits of your workers and add an air of enthusiasm and cheer—and victory—to your campaign.

Telephones

As soon as you have lined up your headquarters, reserve your telephone numbers and set a date for installing the phones and starting the service.

Be sure to get enough lines to handle both incoming and outgoing calls. That will be especially important during the final weeks of the campaign. And, make sure your phone lines are in *rotary*—so that the incoming calls will automatically switch from one line to the next line if the first numbers are busy.

Figure out how many instruments you will need:
—one at the *reception desk*
—one in the *candidate's office*, one in the *chairman's office*, and
—one at each of the desks for *subcommittee chairmen* who work
    at the headquarters (precincts, fund-raising, publicity, etc.)
The candidate and campaign chairman, and probably the finance
chairman, should have *private* (unlisted) numbers in addition to
the regular headquarters lines.
If you plan to use headquarters as a telephone bank to help
on the voter canvass, polling, or get-out-the-vote drives, decide
on the number of extra lines you will need and order them ahead
of time. They can be installed just before the phone brigades go
into operation and can be removed as soon as the calling is completed.

Equipment

Try to get most of your office equipment donated.
Sometimes a friendly office supply company will loan you used
desks and chairs; sometimes a local industry or community group
or church will have some equipment you can borrow. Volunteers
may have some spare tables and chairs they can loan to the campaign.
Be sure to *label each piece* with the owner's name so that it
can all be returned when the campaign is over. And, keep a *complete
inventory* of all equipment—for insurance purposes and your own
peace of mind. Be sure all office equipment is covered under the
fire insurance policy taken out on the headquarters.
This is the type of office equipment needed in the typical headquarters:
—seven or eight *desks*, with *chairs*
—five or six large *tables* (with large, flat work surfaces—the kind
    usually used at church suppers, etc.)
—20 to 30 *folding chairs*
—several fairly nice chairs for the *reception area*—and a coffee

table, some end tables, and a lamp or two, if possible
—*shelves*—for office supplies, campaign materials storage, etc.
—a *mimeograph* or duplicating machine, plus a sturdy *work table*, and a *storage cabinet* for supplies (ink, paper, etc.)
—three or four *typewriters*
—an *adding machine* (and rolls of tape)
—several *filing cabinets* (at least one that can be locked)
—*clothes rack,* or clothes tree,
—*wastepaper baskets* and trash cans, and
—electric *coffee urn* or coffee-making machine (or, in warmer climates, an old refrigerator or softdrink dispenser).

Supplies

As your campaign progresses you will discover what supplies you will need for a smooth operation. Here are some basics that should be on hand when you open the headquarters:
—scratch *pads* and memo pads
—*pens and pencils* (including grease pencils or felt pens)
—*stationery and envelopes*
—*large manila envelopes*
—*file folders* and *file cards* (3″ x 5″)
—several large *appointment calendars*
—plain *typing paper* (regular bond)
—*carbon paper*
—*mimeograph supplies* (ink, paper, correction fluids, stencils, etc.)
—*paper clips* and *rubber bands*
—*staplers and staples*
—*mailing labels* (33 per sheet, perforated and gummed)
—*volunteer pledge cards*
—*contribution pledge cards*
—campaign *literature and materials* (bumper stickers, buttons, etc.)
—*postage stamps or postage meter*
—large *maps of district* showing precinct boundaries
—*thumb tacks, scotch tape,* etc.

Staffing

Your campaign headquarters should be *open six days a week,* Monday through Saturday. At the start of the campaign, the headquarters should be *open during working hours* (9 am to 5 pm); as election day nears, the headquarters should be open in the evening hours. Committee chairmen will want to use the headquarters for meetings of their volunteers, etc. Make sure the meeting times are coordinated to prevent conflicts.

Whenever the headquarters is open, one person should be in charge. If the *headquarters chairman,* or a paid secretary cannot be on hand, someone should be designated as *major domo* of the headquarters facilities (other than the candidate or the general campaign chairman). Be sure the person in charge of the headquarters has been fully briefed on all details and duties, and any special business or event that is planned during the evening.

Most of the work in the headquarters (mailings, checking voter index sheets, making up precinct kits, etc.) will be done by volunteers. Give these folks as much *advance notice* on projects as you can. If a mailing is planned for Thursday, don't wait until Wednesday afternoon to recruit the workers. Try to give them a week's notice—several days, at least.

If, for some reason, a project is delayed or cancelled *be sure to notify the volunteers.* Never waste the time or efforts of a volunteer. Some might have to hire a babysitter, or reserve the family car, or go to extra expense to get the headquarters. Make sure their trip is worthwhile and that there is something for them to do when they arrive.

And, make sure that the various materials for work projects are on hand and ready. Don't wait until the workers arrive to set up the tables or bring in the envelopes or letters or whatever they are to work on. Have everything ready and waiting.

When a project is going to require a large number of extra workers set up a night phone crew to call for volunteers. In that way you will avoid tying up the headquarters phones during the day, and also you will be likely to find more of the volunteers at home (7 pm to 9 pm).

Communications

It is important that the volunteers who work in the campaign headquarters feel they are part of the team effort (they are!) and that they know what is going on in the campaign.

So, communicate!

One way to do that is to have a headquarters *bulletin board.* Use it to post news of the campaign, and keep that news up-to-date.

Items for that board should include:

—*schedule* for the coming week

—*publicity* from local media

—schedule of *candidate's radio and TV appearances*

—*notices and notes* on rallies, parades, etc.

—notices on times and places of *meetings and work sessions*

—announcements of *new committee assignments,* etc.

—general information of interest to campaign personnel.

A good bulletin board is important. Assign some responsible and creative person to keep it *fresh, neat and dynamic.*

Another way to maintain good headquarters communications is to issue a weekly (or, bi-weekly) *bulletin or newsletter.* This need not be fancy—just a few pages mimeographed, giving the latest news on the candidate and the campaign, plus items about campaign personnel. You might also mail this to the precinct workers, to keep them filled in.

Prayer

While we're on the subject of communications . . .

. . . why not start off each day at headquarters with a *prayer time.* You'll be surprised at the difference that will make.

Spend a few moments at the start of the day with The Lord. *Make it an open house* and invite everyone to attend.

It's not a matter of praying for election victory. It's a need to *seek His will and His guidance* in all our efforts. To be still and know that He is God. To put His Kingdom first and to let all things follow in their proper order.

"In all thy ways acknowledge Him, and He will direct thy path."

APPENDIX

II. All About M-O-N-E-Y: Budgets and Fund-Raising

It takes money to run a political campaign. *It sure does!*

Some congressional candidates have spent as much as $250,000 (even more) in their bid for public office. Some candidates for the state legislature have spent almost as much. And, there are cases on record where candidates for a city council seat have spent in access of $100,000!

Federal and state laws have put a crimp in much of that spending and a ceiling on most of those budgets. Now, perhaps, just plain citizens can have a shot at running for public office.

BUDGETS

Unless you, or your candidate, is a millionaire—or you are backed by a well-heeled and high-powered political machine—campaign money is not much different than any other kind of money: *it's hard to come by and it's easy to spend;* it comes in like molasses and it goes outlike water.

That is why a realistic and a detailed budget is essential:
—it will help make sure that you *don't waste money* and that you spend it on those activities and items that will produce the *maximum* results
—it will help you *guard against overspreading* and debt, and
—it will *help your fund-raisers* raise money.

How do you set up a campaign budget?

It's not much different than setting up a budget for most everything else. It's common sense and attention to detail.

Step-by-Step

Let's take each major category (or activity) in the campaign and apply it to the budget. There are about *eight major categories.* As we list them, and detail them, let's assign *budget reference numbers;* they will be useful later on:

1. HEADQUARTERS
    01 Rent
    02 Utilities
    03 Insurance
    04 Telephone
    05 Postage
    06 Equipment
        a. Furniture
        b. Machines
    07 Supplies & Stationery
    08 Signs & Decorations
    09 Miscellaneous (petty cash, etc.)

2. CANDIDATE (personal)
    01 Travel
    02 Telephone
    03 Meals & Exp.

3. STAFF
   01 Salaries & Wages
   02 Taxes & Contributions
   03 Expenses
      a. Travel
      b. Meals

4. PRINTING
   01 Stationery
   02 Campaign literature
   03 Signs & Posters
   04 Bumper stickers, decals, etc.
   05 Precinct materials and forms
   06 Misc. (buttons, etc.)

5. ADVERTISING
   01 Direct Mail
      a. Production
      b. Printing
      c. Postage
      d. Professional services
   02 Radio
      a. Production & Tapes
      b. Time
   03 Television
      a. Production
      b. Time
   04 Newspaper Ads
      a. Production (art, type, photo, etc.)
      b. Space
   05 Billboards
      a. Production (paper)
      b. Boards (showings)

6. PUBLICITY & PRESS RELATIONS
   01 Photography & News Mats
   02 Stationery & Supplies

03 Postage & Delivery
04 Expenses (Entertainment, etc.)

7. RESEARCH & ANALYSIS
   01 Professional Services
   02 Printing
   03 Lists, subscriptions, etc.
   04 Expenses (volunteers, etc.)

8. FUND-RAISING
   01 Stationery & Supplies
   02 Postage
   03 Expense
      a. Travel
      b. Entertainment

9. SPECIAL EVENTS
   01 Rallies, Parades, etc.
   02 Open House, etc.
   03 Misc.

10. MISCELLANEOUS
    01 Contingency Fund

This is a fairly detailed, and expanded, budget. Smaller campaigns will probably not need so much detail; if not, *tailor it to your needs.* But, be sure that your projected budget is *as complete as possible* so that there are no unexpected, last-minute expenses cropping up to throw things out of whack!

Figure The Costs

As precisely as you can, estimate what each item, and each category, will cost. Make the estimates as accurate as possible; find ways to trim those cost wherever you can. By working on the budget with the various committee chairmen involved, you will be able to get a much more accurate projection of costs and totals.

Take the *headquarters* item as an example.

Can the headquarters chairman get a friendly realtor or landlord to donate the campaign headquarters? Or, what about rent at a reduced rate—just enough to cover taxes and insurance?

Let's figure that you can get a ground-floor headquarters site in a good location for $200 a month. If you plan to open the headquarters in March, and run until June, that would be four months at $200—or, $800 rent for the primary campaign. (It will be necessary to create an entirely new budget for the general election—for both operational purposes and campaign spending reports.)

What about *utilities*—light and heat? Is $150 a month a fair estimate? Less at the start and more toward the end, depending on the number of hours and days the headquarters is open each week.

How about *office equipment*—desks, typewriters, etc.? How much can the headquarters chairman (or, perhaps, the campaign chairman) borrow from friendly businessmen, etc.? Can you get what you must rent at a reduced rate? Remember: every dollar you save now can be spent on advertising or printing later in the campaign.

Figure out the *month-by-month costs* for the other categories. Take *postage*, for example. Do you plan to use direct mail? If so, in what month or months? How many pieces do you plan to mail? Will it be a district-wide mailing to every house? Or a mailing to the registered members of your party, only? How do you plan to mail it: first class? Or, third? *Check your local post office.* The folks there can help you with your estimates.

What about *printing*? How many different pieces of campaign literature do you plan? Check with the publicity chairman. How many copies of each? Check the general chairman. If your campaign is strong on volunteer help, you'll need more literature. Be sure to take that into consideration. Don't send your volunteers into the precincts empty-handed!

And, what about *advertising*? What do you plan to spend? In what media? Starting when? If you plan to spend $10,000 in the media, get an *advertising agency*. It won't cost you anything extra;

the agency makes its money from the commissions paid by the media. Have the agency prepare a budget for you—by media, and by month.

If your ad budget is not large enough to warrant the services of an agency, get in touch with the *media representatives*—the ad salesman at the local newspaper, or the time salesman at the radio station. They know their business and they know the market you want to reach. They will be glad to help you set up a budget and a cash flow schedule.

If your state law requires the reporting of "in kind" contributions be sure you keep accurate records of these and their approximate value.

Flow Chart

Now that you have your basic budget fairly well in mind, and the various committee chairmen are in agreement, let's put it all together.

Purchase or make some *"summary"* sheets. You will need at least eight vertical columns. The first column ("Item") should be wider than the others. Print the word *"Total"* at the top of column two, and then print the names of the months at the top of the remaining columns (January through June, for the primary, or June through November, for the general).

Now, list the various categories and items in column one. Use the budget code already set up: Headquarters, for example, is 1; Headquarters rent is 1-01, utilities, 1-02, etc. This may seem bothersome but it will make it easier to keep account of invoices and charges, etc., as the campaign progresses.

Start detailing your campaign budget: in total and by the months. Take the Headquarters category, as an example. Set up that budget for the six months of the primary campaign. Dependent on your actual items and costs, it will look something like this:

1. Headquarters	TOTAL	Jan.	Feb.	Mar.	Apr.	May	June
01 Rent	$ 800.00	—	—	$200	$200	$200	$200
02 Utilities	475.00	—	—	75	100	150	150

03 Insurance	100.00			25	25	25	25
04 Telephone	950.00	–	–	150	250	400	150
05 Equipment	450.00	–	–	50	100	150	150
06 Supplies	550.00		250	25	75	100	100
07 Postage	600.00	25	25	100	150	200	100
08 Signs & Dec.	325.00	–	–	250	25	25	25
09 Misc. (Petty Cash)	400.00	–	–	100	100	100	100
TOTALS	$4,650.00	$25.00	$275	$975	$1025	$1350	$1000

This gives you a fairly clear picture of what the headquarters operation will cost for the six months of the primary. (The figures used above are strictly hypothetical; don't let them influence your calculations.)

Detail the remaining categories and items, just as you have done for Headquarters. If the various committee chairmen have been correct in projecting their schedules and their costs, you will arrive at a comprehensive and accurate budget projection. Be sure that the chairmen refer to their *campaign timetable* (ref. Chapter Twelve) as they work on their particular part of the budget. It is important to pinpoint the needs on some of the major expenses (advertising, postage for direct mail, etc.) so that the money is on hand when it is needed.

Out of Sight?

Suppose you complete the budget and it adds up to more than the committee had planned to spend. Go back and start cutting, piece by piece.

First, eliminate any "frills". It will be a good exercise. Get the chairmen in on the act. It will force them, and you, to really analyze the proposed expenditures and the amounts allocated to the various activities. You will all be forced to concentrate on those items and activities that produce the most for the dollar spent.

After you have cut everywhere you can, without endangering

effective campaign operations, review the situation. Perhaps an increase in the budget is in order. Is that permissible under the existing state or federal laws? And, it is realistic as far as the fund-raisers are concerned?

Remember: every penny spent is a penny that must first be raised So stick to your budget and don't waste your money.

FUND-RAISING

Now that the committee has agreed on the budget, the job is to raise the money.

How do you raise funds for a political campaign? You go out and ask for it.

The late Senator Robert A. Taft once remarked that if you wanted a man's vote, you had to ask him for it. It's the same with a man's campaign contribution. If you want it, *ask for it.* The more outstanding your candidate, the stronger your organization, and the hotter the issues, the better your chances of "getting it".

Finance Chairman

A good finance chairman will have some ideas of his own on how to raise money. Probably he's been down the fund-raising road before.

He will no doubt have some *key contacts* of his own—from past activities. They will be prime prospects. He may want the candidate and/or the campaign chairman to accompany him when he visits these key contacts. And, that's a good way to get started.

But, successful fund-raising depends on more than personal contacts; successful fund-raising also *demands good organization.* And that is where a strong finance committee comes in.

The *finance committee* should include a wide range of leaders from all of the important business, professional, industrial and community groups in the district. Men and women from such fields as:

finance (banking and investments and insurance), *business* (retail and wholesale, goods and services), *industry* (manufacturing, processing, transportation, construction, etc.), *healing arts* (medical, dental, pharmaceutical), *law, engineering, education, agriculture, real estate* and *property development, recreation,* etc.

The finance committee should certainly include *Christian business and professional men and women.* If a Christian agrees to seek public office, Christians in other endeavors should support him.

"Vertical" Committees

The finance committee, as a group, is a powerful instrument for fund-raising. The concerted effort of the individuals on that committee should certainly open many doors and many pocketbooks to the campaign. The very fact that such prominent men and women are serving on the finance committee should, in itself, be worth several thousand dollars—through personal contributions and through the contributions of friends and associates of the committee members. Every member of the finance committee should be able to say, "I gave".

The individuals on the finance committee should also serve as the heads of *subcommittees* to raise money within their particular business, profession or industrial community. These subcommittees are often called "vertical" committees. Each member of the finance committee becomes, in effect, chairman of a "vertical" fund-raising committee. He recruits other members from his particular industry or profession to help him raise that money. Thus, the finance committee is not only a powerful group in itself, it is actually numerous subgroups working—each within its own sphere of influence—to expand the efforts of the whole.

Suppose that one of these vertical committees covers the transportation industry. The chairman and his members invite the leaders of the transportation industry to meet the candidate at a fund-raising lunch. At that luncheon, the candidate and the campaign chairman should be prepared to make a strong and multifaceted presentation:

1. the candidate should present, concisely and with conviction,

his *basic political philosophy* and his views on some of the *important legislation or governmental regulations* that are of prime importance to the transportation industry

2. the campaign chairman should give a *realistic and penetrating appraisal of the campaign* and a preview of campaign strategy, and

3. a *review of the campaign budget* (detailed by category and item, and cash flow requirements)

4. the hosts of the luncheon then make *a strong appeal for campaign contributions.*

If each "vertical" committee would hold such a luncheon, and make such an appeal for campaign funds, a large portion of the budget could be raised without too much difficulty.

Similar luncheons, or receptions, can be employed to solicit *smaller* but nevertheless important campaign contributions from other groups. The key, of course, is to have the gathering hosted by a prominent member, or members, of the profession or group involved—and to have one or more of the hosts make a strong appeal for campaign contributions from those present. The candidate is important to the overall meeting but he should *not* be expected to act as a fund-raiser. Let others attend to those duties

Direct Mail

Direct mail is becoming increasingly more important in fund raising. If you break even in your first mailing, you can still make money later in the campaign with a follow-up mailing. For example, suppose you mail out 10,000 letters early in the campaign at a cost of $1,500. Suppose you receive 200 responses with an average contribution of $10 for a total of $2,000. You went to a lot of work for only $500. *However,* suppose that one month before the end of the campaign, you mail again to the 200 respondents. It will cost $30 and you may receive another 150 responses at a $10 average. That's a total of $1500. You have just made $1470 ($1500-$30). In addition to the financial benefits you have brought people into closer contact with the campaign. A man who gives money is more apt to vote, more apt to urge his friends to vote for you.

There are, basically, two types of direct mail:
—the *personal letter,* and
—the *mass-mailing effort.*

In the first—the personal letter—the writer knows the person to whom he, or she, is writing well enough to urge support of the candidate and expect that this will have some impact.

This is the type of letter the finance chairman might write to close business associates, urging them to contribute to the candidate's campaign. It is also the type of letter that one Christian family might write to another, asking them to join in the campaign.

Some individuals—those who are well established in a profession or business, or those who have been active in church work or in politics for a number of years—have large personal mailing lists. On very special occasions, they will write to solicit help for a cause or a candidate. Such letters are usually quite productive.

Mass-Mailings

Mass-mail can be quite productive. Returns will depend on:
—the type of *lists* that are used
—the strength (pulling power) of the *letter*
—the *material* included in the mailing, and
—the *type of appeal* being made (a well-known and worthy cause, an emotional issue, a prominent and respected candidate, etc.)

Lists

Where do you get good lists for direct mail?
Traditional sources include the local chambers of commerce, trade and professional association, country club, fraternal and service organization rosters, PTA membership lists, contributors to previous fund-raising campaigns, subscription lists to special publications, etc.

Since the candidate is a Christian, one of the best mailing lists would be the *names and addresses of the Christian* families in the district. Campaign committee members should be able to assemble such a list by working with their friends in the various congregations, contacting friendly pastors and church secretaries, members of various Christian organizations and Bible classes and similar groups. If some of these organizations will not release their membership lists, perhaps they will do the mailing if you will supply the materials and pay the postage.

Christmas Card Lists

One of the most effective mailing lists is your own *Christmas card list.*

Get every member of the candidate's committee—all the precinct workers, and all of their friends, and all the volunteers and their friends—to write to the folks on their Christmas card list. Send the folks on those lists a short letter, pointing out that the candidate is a Christian, and that he deserves their support and their help. Explain why he is running for office, and what he believes in and why he is well-qualified for the post. Urge friends and their families to help. Enclose a pledge card and return envelope.

Make sure it is a personal letter—do not send a printed letter. *It's the personal touch that makes all the difference!"*

Letters

The letter used in the direct mail appeal should be strong, and to the point. It should present the *clear and compelling reasons* why the potential contributor should support the candidate and the cause, and why he should contribute money to the campaign. Make the letter a "grabber".

In addition to the letter, which should be personalized, send a piece of the candidate's literature (an attractive, easy-to-read folder) and a *return envelope:* make it as easy as possible for the potential contributor to give.

And, a suggestion: enclose with your letter a chart showing what various campaign contributions will pay for. For once, give the contributor an idea of what his money will do for the campaign.

With all this talk about thousands and millions of dollars in political campaigns, the average citizen wonders what one dollar can buy, or what good it does. Well, show him. Figure out how many *campaign brochures* you can get for one dollar, or five dollars. How many *bumper stickers* can you get for ten dollars? How big an ad in the local paper for $25? Work out a chart, something like this:

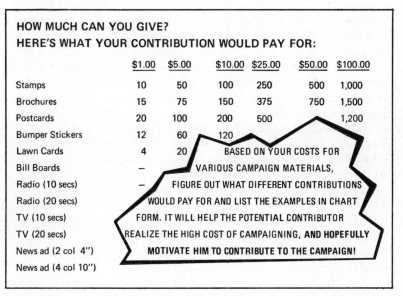

HOW MUCH CAN YOU GIVE?
HERE'S WHAT YOUR CONTRIBUTION WOULD PAY FOR:

	$1.00	$5.00	$10.00	$25.00	$50.00	$100.00
Stamps	10	50	100	250	500	1,000
Brochures	15	75	150	375	750	1,500
Postcards	20	100	200	500		1,200
Bumper Stickers	12	60	120			
Lawn Cards	4	20				
Bill Boards	–					
Radio (10 secs)	–					
Radio (20 secs)						
TV (10 secs)						
TV (20 secs)						
News ad (2 col 4")						
News ad (4 col 10")						

BASED ON YOUR COSTS FOR VARIOUS CAMPAIGN MATERIALS, FIGURE OUT WHAT DIFFERENT CONTRIBUTIONS WOULD PAY FOR AND LIST THE EXAMPLES IN CHART FORM. IT WILL HELP THE POTENTIAL CONTRIBUTOR REALIZE THE HIGH COST OF CAMPAIGNING, **AND HOPEFULLY MOTIVATE HIM TO CONTRIBUTE TO THE CAMPAIGN!**

Dinners

Almost every political campaign holds at least one *fund-raising* dinner. The question is, how much to charge? If you charge too much, you eliminate some staunch supporters who can't afford the high prices. If you charge too little, you don't make any money for the campaign. So, should you charge $100? Or, $50? Or, how much?

If you are going to have a fund-raising dinner, *have a fund-raising dinner*. Charge $100. You may not get a large attendance but remember this: if you sell 300 tickets to a $100 dinner, you should clear at least $25,000. It would take at least 700 tickets to a $50 dinner to net the same amount. (And, you probably couldn't sell 700 tickets!)

Just remember: putting on a fund-raising dinner takes a lot of work and worry and planning and follow-through and sales effort. Figure on at least 90 days of hard work: *90 days.* That is the amount of time you will need to line up a good speaker, get the tickets printed, *and sold,* reserve the site, arrange the menu, line up the entertainment, *sell the tickets,* send out the invitations to the VIPS, generate publicity, *get the tickets sold,* take care of the table decorations, have the program printed, *sell tickets,* line up the head table guests, recruit the hostesses, *sell tickets,* arrange for parking attendants, *and get the tickets sold!*

But, if it's a success—and you make $25,000 (or, even $10,000)—it's worth it; if it's a flop, it's a real bummer.

Family Affairs

Many campaigns go ahead and hold the big, fancy $100 a plate dinner (to raise money) and then hold one or two low-cost family affairs (to raise some money but, more importantly, to generate enthusiasm and go-power for the campaign).

Have a ball! Pick a hall—the Elks, or the Sons of Italy, or the Grange, or American Legion. Have a simple menu: spaghetti, chili, a Mexican Dinner, fried chicken from the Colonel's, or whatever. One 1974 candidate for Congress held a $5.00 dinner and served food purchased at the local hamburger stand for $1.00 a head. It was a great success.

Line up some good amateur entertainment. *Hold down on the speeches.* Have a community song fest. Charge maybe five bucks a plate or *$10 for the family.* It will be a night to remember.

Better yet, have a *pot-luck dinner.* Every family bring something.

Serve buffet-style, on paper plates, with paper cups for the coffee and punch for the kids. Pound cake by the square yard and salad by the bucket. Charge $2.50. Or, make it $5.00 for the family. *It's all clear profit.* And, if you promote it properly, you'll have a crowd and clear several hundred dollars—probably close to $500.

Do that several times during the campaign, in different parts of the district. With different menus and entertainment. It's a good fund-raiser and a great fun-raiser. It will make friends and help win elections.

Pledges Are Great!

Some folks will want to contribute to the campaign but they will be up to their eyebrows in monthly payments—house mortgage,

CONTRIBUTOR'S PLEDGE CARD (4" x 6")

TO: _____ for _____ Committee

      P.O. Box _____
      Hometown, U.S.A.

Yes! I want to help elect _____ to the _____ .
I will pledge $_____ to be payable on or before _____ and
I will contribute $_____ per month from _____
    through_____ . Enclosed is my first check
    for $_____ .

Last Name	First Name

Address	Phone

Have enough of these printed to supply the Finance Chairman and the members of his Finance Committee. Also, estimate the quantity that will be required for fund-raising meetings, direct mail, etc.

car installment, furniture, church tithe, etc. So, they won't be able to give as much to the campaign as they'd like to—at least not in one lump sum.

But, they would be willing to *pledge so much a month*—say $5.00. Is that okay? *You bet!* The more the merrier. Make sure the pledge card provides several different ways for folks to support the campaign financially. And, if they want a friendly reminder each month, you can handle that, too. Just have a supply of file cards run off with a *pledge-jogger* and send it to those who slide behind now and then.

After all, five dollars a month is five dollars a month. If you have a hundred families doing that—it adds up; it's $3,000 over a six-month period!

Young Folks

Don't forget the young people. They can raise money, too! And, they'll do it, if you'll encourage them.

There are any number of projects they can handle:
—*car washes, bake and cake sales, rummage sales, yard and garage sales, and on and on.*

It all brings in money and it helps make the young folks an important part of the campaign—and, they should be!

Use Your Ads

Whenever you run an ad—in the newspaper or on the air—*solicit campaign contributions.* Just come right out and ask the readers, or the listeners, to send in a campaign contribution. Tell them you need the money; that it's a people's campaign and there are no big wheelers and dealers putting up the money—it's a dime-and-dollar program.

You'd be surprised how much money you'll get. Not enough to finance the campaign—but maybe enough to help pay for the cost of those ads.

And, you might consider putting a *fund-raiser box* at the end of all your campaign literature. It's a good touch. Will it bring in any money? You'll never know till you try!

Make your fund-raising efforts as *broad-based* as possible. The more people you have supporting your effort, the stronger your campaign will be. It's better to have 1,000 citizens giving $10 a piece than to have ten persons putting up $1,000 each.

It's still a fact of political life: *the fellow who puts $5.00 into your campaign will be out there pulling for your candidate all the way!*

APPENDIX

III. Scheduling Aids

A. CONFIRMATION FORM

(Use this or a similar form to confirm that the candidate will speak before a group that has invited him to appear. The form should be made in triplicate: one copy to the program chairman of the group that extended the invitation; one copy to the candidate or campaign chairman, and one copy to be kept in the scheduling chairman's file.)

To confirm our acceptance of your kind invitation:

_____ (name of candidate) _____ will speak

to _____ (name of group) _____

at _____ (meeting place and address) _____

on _____(day, date) _____ at _____ (time) _____am/pm

The title of _____ (candidate's name) _____ talk will be:

_____

The time required for the presentation is _____ minutes.

There will ( ) will not ( ) be a question and answer period following the talk.

There will ( ) will not ( ) be other speakers on the program.

The candidate will ( ) will not ( ) require transportation to ( ) and from ( ) your meeting. Details of arrival time, pick up point, etc., are attached.

The candidate will be accompanied by _____, and will ( ) will not ( ) stay for the entire program.

To make sure that the candidate can do the best possible job for your organization, we would appreciate the following:

( ) lectern or podium   ( ) public address system
( ) easel for charts   ( ) film projector and screen
( ) stand for flip charts   _____ (type) _____

For the convenience of your program and publicity chairman, a copy of suggested introductory remarks and a copy of the candidate's biographical sketch are attached.

If there are any questions, please call. And, again, thank you!

B. SPEAKER'S DETAIL SHEET

(Use this or a similar form to record all pertinent details about the candidate's speaking engagement. Make a detail sheet on each and every scheduled appearance. Be sure to include all information that is of importance. Fill out in triplicate: one copy for the candidate, one for the campaign chairman and one for the scheduling chairman.)

_____ (name of organization) _____ Date: _____

Time: ___ am/pm

Address: _____ (Room name or number) _____

_____ (Name of building or site) _____

_____ (Street and number, etc.) _____

_____ (City or Town) _____

Location and number of nearest telephone: _____

_____

Directions: _____

_____(route, how to get there, etc.) _____
_____

A map of the route is ( ) attached.
Contact: _____
Phone Number:_____
Individual who will meet candidate at event: _____
Individual who will introduce candidate: _____
VIPS at headtable: _____
_____

Expected attendance _____ (number) _____.
Type of group: _____ (main interests) _____
Title (or topic) of remarks: _____
Question & answers ( ) Yes   ( ) No.
Others on program: _____
_____

Remarks: _____
_____

IV. The A B Cs Of Statistical Analysis

By analyzing precinct registration and voting patterns over a period of years it is possible to obtain a fairly accurate evaluation of political climate and vote potential.

This is generally known as statistical (vote) analysis and it can provide information of real value to the campaign. The information is especially valuable if you do not have sufficient manpower to cover all of your precincts and must decide which precincts deserve priority emphasis for maximum results.

Materials Needed

These are the materials needed to make a statistical analysis of the precincts in your district:

1. *a list of all the precincts* and the *voter registration data* in all of those precincts for the election years to be studied. This

list can usually be obtained from the county clerk or registrar of voters. If the clerk will not allow the records to be removed from the office, volunteers can be assigned to copy the information.

PRECINCT VOTE ANALYSIS

PRECINCT #_____   Pri   Gen

PRIORITY		

	Dem.	Rep.	Other	Total	±
19__ Registr.					
Pres.					
Congress					
Legis.					
19__ Registr.					
Pres.					
Congress					
Legis.					
19__ Registr.					
Pres.					
Congress					
Legis.					

(Legis. = vote for state legislative district)
($\mp$ = number of votes by which your party won or lost race)
MOST RECENT REGISTRATION DATA: (Date_____)
   Democrat _____   Republican_____
   Independent_____   Other_____
                  Total_____

2. *an abstract (or certified record) of the votes cast* in each of the precincts for each of the selected elections (refer to the sample Precinct Vote Analysis sheet). These voting records can be obtained from the county clerk or registrar of voters.
3. *a map of the district* showing the precinct boundaries. Obtain such a map from your county engineer, or county clerk. Perhaps your party headquarters already has such a map; if so, try to borrow it and make your own copy.
4. *a supply of Precinct Vote Analysis sheets* (see sample form). Mimeograph enough of these sheets to have at least two for each precinct; use one as a work sheet on the precinct and the other for your final analysis report.

Gathering The Data

Using a vote analysis sheet, compile the data for each of the elections in each of the precincts for each of the years involved. This will involve quite a bit of research work. As suggested in *Chapter Seven,* recruit as many volunteers as possible to help on this project.

It is recommended that the analysis include at least three recent election years, and at least three types of races plus the basic registration figures. Refer to the sample vote analysis sheet for more detail.

Here is a sample of how the 1974 election data might look for one precinct:

	Dem.	Rep.	Other	Total	±
Registration	152	102	32	286	+50
U. S. Senator	106	76	6	188	+30
Congress	98	84	4	186	+14
Governor	76	97	3	176	−21
State Legis.	63	81	–	144	−18

(In the column headed "±" enter the margin by which the candidate of your party won or lost in that precinct. For the sake of illustration in the above example, the Democratic margins are shown.)

Record the election and registration data for each of the selected election years in each precinct. *Complete a vote analysis sheet for each precinct in the district.* This will give you a picture of the voting habits and patterns in each precinct for the years you have selected.

If you want a picture of the voting habits for the entire district, prepare an *analysis map.* This is done by using the vote for either the congressional or legislative race in the most recent election. Color each precinct, using three shades of two colors (one color for each party; blue for Democrats and red for Republican):

Dark shade—party carried precinct by 50 votes or more

Medium shade—party carried precinct by 21 to 50 votes

Light shade—party carried precinct by less than 20 votes.

Putting The Analysis To Work

The purpose of the analysis is to find out "where the ducks are"—where the precinct workers can get the maximum results for their efforts.

The "ducks" your precinct people will be going after in the primary are different from those you will be going after in the general election. In the primary, *only those voters registered in your party* can vote for your candidate; thus, you concentrate on the voters in your party.

Let's try and figure out how many votes you will need to win the primary.

How many voters are registered in your party in your district?
_____

What percentage of them traditionally vote in the primary? _____ (The county clerk can supply that statistic for you, or you can figure it out by checking past election data.)

Multiply the registration total by the percentage of turnout. That should give you an approximation of the number of voters in your party who will vote in the primary: _____ *Make fifty-five percent of that your target.* Go after that total—even if there are more than two candidates splitting up the party vote in the primary.

Priority In The Primary

Now that you know how many votes you need, where are you going to get them?

You get them in the precincts, through precinct work. Your precinct workers go hunting "where the ducks are" and in the primary those ducks are the voters registered in your party.

Thus, you concentrate in those precincts with the highest number of party members.

For example, a precinct in which 70-75% of the registered voters are members of your party would be *a priority precinct.* That's where you would be sure to have *at least one coffee* for the candidate. That's where you would be sure to have a *strong precinct organization*—with as many blockworkers as possible. That's where you would really work hard to canvass the voters, sell *your* candidate, and deliver *your* votes on election day.

By contrast, a precinct in which 70-75% of the registered voters were members of the opposition party would be a low-low priority precinct in the primary. Try and recruit a precinct captain there—to be sure. And, try to get out your vote there—you bet. But, don't waste any extra effort there; save your extra effort and use it when those ducks are.

Thus, to establish precinct priorities for the primary contest, rank the precincts in order of party registration:

the greater the party registration, the higher the priority.

Mark that priority—either using the percentage figure or a code (A, B, C, etc.) in the *space provided* in the upper righthand corner of the vote analysis sheet. When you have ranked all of the precincts for the primary, make up a list (starting with the top priority down through the lowest) for the campaign precinct chairman. That list will be used to recruit and deploy precinct workers in the primary.

General Election

Let's suppose that you won the primary. Now, how many votes do you need to win the general election? And, where do you get them?

First, the estimated vote for the general election..

What are the *registration figures* for your party? For the opposition?

What's the *estimated voter turnout?* It will be higher in the general than in the primary. What are the predictions? Sixty-five percent? Seventy? Seventy-three? Republicans usually turn out more of their voters than do the Democrats. Will that be true this time?

How many voters in your party will *cross party lines* and vote for the opposition candidate? Subtract those votes from your party total. Add them to the opposition's.

Do the same thing with the opposition vote. Figure the total turnout, the crossover, and the net base vote. How do the parties and the candidates stack up?

To give you an idea of how these data might look in your district, let's take a hypothetical legislative district. Suppose it comprises 115,000 registered voters: 60,000 Democrats, 40,000 Republicans, 10,000 Independents and 5,000 in the minor parties. Based on past voting patterns indicated by the vote analysis, this is how the projections might look:

	Dem.	Rep.	Ind.	Other	Total
Registered	60,000	40,000	10,000	5,000	115,000
Est. turnout	65%	71%	68%	70%	67.5%
Total vote	39,000	28,400	6,800	3,500	77,700
% Crossover	15%	7%			
Net crossover vote	−3,862	+3,862			
Net base vote [a]	35,138	32,262			

[a] No attempt has been made to distribute the Independent vote. This varies by area. Check election data for your district.

Which Precincts?

In the hypothetical district, the Republicans happen to be short 2,876 votes before they start. Or, if you prefer, the Democrats have a built-in cushion of 2,876 votes. For the sake of discussion, let's suppose that you are the chairman of a Republican campaign in

the district. How would you go about overcoming that deficit?
All is far from lost. You have at least *three ways to go:*
1. persuade at least 1,440 *Democrats to switch* and vote for your candidate
2. increase the *Republican turnout* by at least four percentage points (that would give you some 2,800 extra votes)
3. shoot for at least *70 percent of the Independent vote.* That would require an all-out effort to "sell" the independents on your candidate.

And, of course, you can work in all three of those areas and try to win by gaining some of each.

Whatever you do, most of it will be done in the precincts and the big question is: *which precincts?*

That is where the vote analysis can be your lifesaver. It can point out the best precincts.

First, *study the analysis sheets.* In which precincts is there the greatest opportunity to get Democrats to vote Republican? Past elections will show you that. These will be the *swing precincts,* the ones where Republicans with a little extra effort can convince a sizable number of Democrats to "vote for the man, not the party".

Look for precincts that have been won and lost by five percent or less. Are these your swing precincts? The precincts where you can have the best opportunity to convert Democrats—at least for this one election?

Don't waste your time in precincts where the registration is heavily against you. That usually means a solid opposition and a strong opposition machine or deeply embedded voting habits.

Find your swing precincts and put your effort there. Get the candidate in there for several coffees. Be sure to invite the Democrats. Try and enlist the aid of several Democrats to help in your precinct work—calling or contacting fellow Democrats, lining up a coffee for the candidate, etc. *Remember:* every time you get a member of the opposition party to vote for your candidate, *it's worth two votes*—one more for your candidate, one less for the opponent.

Use much the same technique in going after those Independent voters. Use both the statistical analysis and your precinct canvass sheets to find them, tab those precincts—and go after those voters.

Statistical analysis has helped you find your ducks. It has indicated where you should concentrate your precinct efforts—and suggested the type of approach that will reap the best harvest in the various precincts.

It's up to you and your campaign organization to do the rest.

APPENDIX

V. Suggested References And Reading Materials

Political Action

AFL-CIO Committee on Political Education (COPE), *How To Win, Handbook For Political Education.* 815 16th St., N.W., Washington, D. C. 20006 $5.00

Cannon, James M., Editor, *Politics U.S.A.,* Doubleday, 1960.

Parkinson, Hank. *Winning Your Campaign: A Nuts-and Bolts Guide to Political Victory,* Prentice Hall

Chamber of Commerce of the United States, *Action Course in Practical Politics.* Public Affairs Dept. 1615 H Street, N.W., Washington, D. C. 20006

Shadegg, Stephen C., *How to Win an Election,* Taplinger, 1964

Basic Political Philosophy

THE LAW, Bastiat, Foundation for Economic Education (FEE),
Irvington-on-Hudson, N.Y., 10533
THE CHRISTIAN IN SOCIETY, Earle E. Cairns, Moody Press
ECONOMICS IN ONE EASY LESSON, Henry Hazlitt, Harper
& Brothers, 1946
THE MAINSPRING OF HUMAN PROGRESS, Henry Grady
Weaver, Foundation for Economic Education, Irvington-on-
Hudson, N.Y., 10533
THE NATURE OF THE AMERICAN SYSTEM, Rousas J. Rush-
doony, Craig Press
THE CONSTITUTION OF LIBERTY, F. A. Hayek, Univ. of
Chicago Press.
*THE CHRISTIAN HISTORY OF THE CONSTITUTION OF
THE UNITED STATES,* Verna M. Hall, Foundation for Ameri-
can Christian Education

Periodicals

THE FREEMAN, Foundation for Economic Education, Irvington-
on-Hudson, N.Y. 10533
CHRISTIANITY TODAY, 1014 Washington Bldg., Washington,
D.C. 20005
HUMAN EVENTS, 422 First St., S.E. Washington, D.C. 20003